HOLDING UP
THE SKY

INTERGENERATIONAL LESSONS
OF FATHERHOOD

Tim EJ Campbell

Holding Up the Sky: Intergenerational Lessons of Fatherhood

Copyright © 2025 by Tim EJ Campbell

For permissions, inquiries, or bulk orders, please contact:

Tim EJ Campbell

timcampbellphd@gmail.com

www.holdingupthesky.net

Published 2025

Paperback ISBN: 979-8-9926187-0-9

Printed in the United States

To my parents, Eldon and Wanda, in loving memory.

To my wife, Linda, my confidante, my inspiration, my love.

To my brother, Kent.

To my children, Alana, Kathryn, and Eric, who continue to inspire me to write stories.

ACKNOWLEDGMENTS

I wish to thank Linda and my children for their patience and endless help during the preparation of this book.

Thanks also to Marley Castillo for her excellent advice and counsel on storytelling and writing. I am grateful to my peers—Bill Falcone, Bob Glantz, and Sheila Kogan of the Domingo Writers Group, and to Alon Shalev and his colleagues in the Berkeley Writers Circle. I am also in debt to long-time dear friends, Sandy Vatalaro, Wendy Eisner, and Richard Little, for reading and commenting on the manuscript at various stages. Thanks also to Barton Evans and Jon Frederickson for their friendship, to Lindsay Newton for her insightful comments and excellent suggestions, and to Damon Bradley for kindly providing me with the text of the Marbury Award presentation. Thanks to Lindsey Newton, Kristen Tatroe, and Kristen Caven for their excellent editing. And many thanks to Ralph Scott of Squeaky Cheese Productions and Jamie Bridges at A Room with a View Studios in Petaluma, California.

TABLE OF CONTENTS

PROLOGUE

When a son becomes a father, he has to solve a riddle about the rules of fatherhood. A new father needs to make corrections to the rules handed down from his father, and in making those corrections, he creates a new puzzle for his son.

My dad's rules reflected a hard-scrabble life when he was a kid. By the time I had entered my teen years, his way of fatherhood had crystallized into a suburban version of military commands. His rough style smothered his love under emotional sandpaper and stirred in me a deep disquiet.

One day when I was fifteen, Dad's car wouldn't start. He was already late for work. I sat next to him as the stubborn engine failed to catch. He grew agitated. After many attempts to get it started, his red face was underlined with wetness around his collar. He jumped out and brought a gas can from the garage, thrust it at me, and ordered me to pour gas directly into the carburetor while he turned the engine over. He wasn't making a polite request.

He cranked the engine. I started to pour, hand trembling. A gash of flame erupted from the carburetor toward the gas can I was holding. The bright flash and the smell of combusted fuel shot a spike of fear through me. I flung away the can, terrified. That wasn't the first, or last, time Dad acted recklessly, and I vowed then to not be that kind of dad.

Over the ensuing decades, I nurtured my growing sense of manhood and strengthened my vow. I felt a glowing warmth as my first daughter became a toddler. I aimed to be softer, more open, more trusting—and saw my plan was working. I reveled in the utter joy of fatherhood. Then our second was hospitalized as a newborn with a viral infection of the heart. She wasn't expected to live. She did, but with multiple disabilities. Our third child showed up with a serious hearing loss. Family life morphed from a pleasant dream into an unrecognizable drama.

That's when I began to question my vow. Could I be the soft and loving dad, protecting my family from bad things, when hour after hour, day after day, my wife and I had to contend with the tangled unpredictability of a chaotic, asymmetric family? Under the pressures of disabilities in the family, I sometimes regressed to be like my dad. I was becoming the father I had vowed not to be. Worse, I was creating new problems that my son would have to solve if and when he was to become a father.

This memoir traces my quest for rules that would work for three kids: two disabled, two gifted. (Yes, three kids—one is both). And by work, I mean to carry through, to see them into adulthood. The story traces the complicated dynamic of multi-generational traumas—my father's broken family in the Depression, my own disabled kids, my stumbling efforts to keep things straight, and my son's skepticism about becoming a father. All of us have stories that entail something extraordinary—traumatic events, emotional challenges, family tensions—surprises fathers are never prepared for. Fathering, like mothering, always involves walking into the unknown, using templates designed for the past that must be revised for the present. Yet confronting the chaos and searching for solutions reveal commonalities that bind us together in what it means to be human.

The vortex of disabilities in our family nearly swallowed my wife and me. We struggled often to regain our balance as mother and father, husband and wife. The impulses we followed were ones we learned from our respective fathers, who had decidedly different approaches to life and parenthood. And those early models of fathering led us to collide over how best to father and mother our kids. But deep inside we shared a mutual commitment to learn from our pasts. While many books have been written about mothering, this one is about fathering, how we become fathers, what we learn from our fathers, what we must unlearn, and what we learn about ourselves in this journey of discovery into what is known as fathering.

PART I

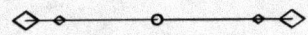

TROUBLES

LIGHTNING STRIKES

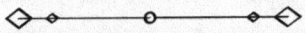

As if by multiple strikes of lightning, fires sprouted simultaneously in numerous places north of San Francisco in the summer of 2018. Strong winds pushed flames racing across two counties, spreading an ominous gray haze that covered the sky for forty miles. A haunting image from a local newspaper showed a father holding his child's hand, watching from a distance as their home went up in smoke. That wrenching image of father and son captured so much about fatherhood in my life.

For one thing, the photo made me think of my own father. In 1919, at the age of five, he watched from a distance as his family's farmhouse and barn were eaten up by flames. His father raced frantically to contain the fire. That catastrophe for my dad set in motion a chain of events around fathering that stretched across generations, affecting me and my children, and reaching right up to the moment of writing these words.

* * *

My aunt Vera, the fourth oldest of my father's eight

brothers and sisters, told me the story of the fire. Normally, Vera possessed a calm, unruffled demeanor. The day of my father's funeral, her big brown eyes were doleful and dilated, a hint of moisture forming. In her mid-seventies, she was still an original Earth Mother: soft-spoken, never hurried, with a lap that could cuddle a dozen puppies.

A spiritual calm hung around her.

On the afternoon of the fire, Vera recalled, she and the other children were frightened by panicked shouting that broke the afternoon calm. They caught the sharp smell and light crackle of burning hay. The shifting dance of white smoke swirled up into the bright blue sky. The fire was spreading quickly, lapping up the dry barn wood.

"I didn't realize that the fire had reached the barn," she recalled. Her tone was matter of fact—understandable after some sixty years—but the pain still floated on her words. "Your grandmother told me to take the youngest ones into the field." She paused, looking up at the sky, remembering being a seven-year-old child. "I was carrying Ivan." My uncle was then just three months. "Then I grabbed your father's hand." She paused to silently calculate. "Your dad was five. I hurried out the back." She paused again, as if watching the rerun in slow motion in her mind. "Mother gathered the others."

While the family fled to safe ground, my grandfather crashed frantically through the chaos in the corral on the Northern California farm where he was foreman. His focus was on his horses, his livelihood, the only asset that would allow him to recover after the fire. Smoke billowed out the barn openings. He threw open yard gates and made his way across the paddock. His overalls, already soaked from the exceptional summer heat that year, stuck to his torso. He ignored the cows and goats. The wisps of smoke had driven the cloven hooves into mini-stampedes, and the chickens whirled underfoot like so many miniature, feathered typhoons. The drayage horses were panicked in the barn, impossible to control.

"We sat in a circle in the alfalfa field and watched in tears," Vera said.

I imagined my aunt Vera, sitting with two of her brothers, watching their home and much of what might have been a prosperous future go up in smoke.

"It was your uncle, Happy," Vera said. My Uncle Happy grew up and earned his nickname because of an ever-present grin. "He looked so much like your father." She gazed at me, shaking her head. "He got a cigarette from one of the ranch hands. He was only eight, but I think he never got over the guilt of starting the fire. He covered it up with that always-happy look."

"I think my father never got over the trauma," I said. "He faced life with a frown."

Small wonder, after the fire, the family split up. My grandfather made his way back to timber camps to start over, first as a lumberjack and later, hoping to gain horses, to work as a teamster, to haul cut trees out of the mountains to the mill, or sawn logs out of the mill to lumber yards in towns like Weed and Bend, Oregon. My grandmother returned to Gridley, refusing to raise her kids in a mill town. He sent money sporadically but came back only rarely to visit. They later had more children, but they never again lived together. The Depression finished off their hopes for restoring a family farm.

The image of the father in the North Bay fire also reminded me of myself forty years ago, holding my infant child's hand in a hospital as she lay near death from a mysterious virus that attacked her heart. Petrified and numb from shock, I stood on the edge of panic about how to handle the sudden onset of the disease and the terrible repercussions her illness portended not only for her, but for my oldest daughter, Alana, then three.

Alana had arrived not with a lightning strike, but with a lullaby. She was delivered in a homey setting, an alternative birth center, our first forays into creating a soft, attentive parenthood, distinct from the defensive crouch that had characterized my own father's style, a coarse and resentful style that I wanted to reject, to reinvent.

Linda and I cherished those postpartum hours with Alana, the three of us lying together in bed, Alana nursing while holding my pinky. The week of her birth, I recall crossing the street, thinking to myself over and over, *I'm a father. I'm no longer just a guy, a young man, a doctoral student, a husband. I'm a father and determined to build a new model of fatherhood.* The new version was ready at any moment to jump into an exchange with my daughter. We were going to be close, to teach each other. I was going to show her about loving language and life, and she would signal me about how my fathering was working.

Having a second child three years later seemed natural. We lived a dream and wanted to extend it indefinitely. Linda became pregnant and was due to give birth when Alana reached three-

and-a-half. We thought the timing gave Alana just enough space to form her identity and be comfortable with a little sibling.

Kathryn was born in two hours flat. I lay on a gurney across a short distance in the delivery room from where Linda was recovering. I called over quietly, a sense of contentment in my voice. "We are parents again."

She murmured a soft reply. "Another girl. And did you see how she looked around the room?"

"Yes, she is another special one." I paused. "The doctor was amazed at her alertness."

We named her Kathryn, after two grandmothers, one on each side of the family.

A week later, a friend snapped a photo of the four of us, the only photo we have of the whole family, healthy.

TO THE HOSPITAL

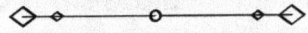

Though Kathryn's arrival was smooth and fast, a week later, mysterious spots appeared on her back. Hospital tests ruled out obvious concerns, like meningitis. We retreated to home, tamping down our fears. We cherished quiet time with our new babe. The tenth day, a Friday, seemed just a quiet afternoon at home. Alana had run next door to play with neighbors. I puttered in the living room, fixing blinds on the windows. Linda entered, a little stiff, her voice tight, her face in a worried knot.

"Something's not right." Linda has always been the first to pick up the faintest signs of trouble, and she was acutely sensitive to Kathryn. "Her breathing is labored." She was holding Kathryn, who showed a primitive stress on her tiny face. I took her while Linda called our pediatrician, who lived down the street.

We sensed something menacing was in the air, but it floated out there beyond our grasp threatening our baby, and we were helpless. Waiting for the doctor to arrive, I held Kathryn's face close to mine. Her mouth opened slightly. She gazed up into my face, but with the unfocused stare of a newborn. Her breathing grew more strained. Her head was laid back, mouth open, airways clear. Yet she made tiny gasping sounds. My gut vibrated with anxiety and helplessness. My dreamy foray into parenting was turning into a nightmare. The pediatrician arrived. She took Kathryn with authority and examined her, listening intently and pushing her fingers into Kathryn's tiny midsection. She finished abruptly, looked up at me, and said: "Get her to the hospital . . . I'll call ahead." She paused; her face tightened and her tone changed: "She might not make it."

I stared at her. My pulse quickened. Internal alarms began building. She spoke softly but her words hit me like a thunderclap. I glanced at Linda. Her face was frozen. The glint of fear we had suppressed waiting for the pediatrician flashed into panic.

"You go," Linda said.

With that word, I understood that Linda needed to stay with Alana. I swept up Kathryn in a single motion and was out the door, moving with dumb determination. I held her close, murmuring encouraging words, as if they would stave off whatever evil seemed to be so nearby. I strapped her into her car seat, mounted backwards next to me in our Datsun, and pulled onto Claremont, heading for the hospital. Her breathing grew more erratic. Her infant face craned upward, confused, distressed. She gasped for air.

I was in a race against something dark and foreboding. The world shrank. Speeding through the streets, I raised my voice and spoke to Kathryn with as much calm encouragement as I could muster. "Hold on, Kathryn, hold on. We'll be there in a minute. Daddy's with you, honey." I was pleading with my baby as though she were a warrior in a battlefield ambulance. I didn't know what else to do.

I kept waiting for some miraculous sign of relief. There was none. I struggled to keep my voice under control; it was all I had to show her she wasn't alone.

"Don't let go. Hold on, Kathryn, hold on."

I pulled up to the emergency entrance and grabbed her out of the car seat, leaving the car sitting in the driveway, doors open. I sprinted through the entrance.

Children's Hospital was a familiar sight from previous visits. I knew exactly where to go. I did not bother to stop at registration or security.

"Baby Campbell," I called out as I rushed past. They had gotten the message and waved me through.

In pediatric intensive care, tiny infants—some under hoods, others strapped onto small tables, still others in small beds—ringed the perimeter of the large room. Each infant patient was heavily shrouded in electro-medical technology. All our earlier visits had been to a pediatric ward where children moved and cried. In intensive care, the tiny infants lay still, heads turned aside, silently acquiescing to the imperatives of tubing and wires. Monitors and lights beeped and blinked.

In the center of the room stood a small table under a bank of lights, fresh linens draped over its edges. Assorted medical paraphernalia hung from rolling stands and ceiling fixtures. Four nurses moved into position, poised around the table. They were expecting us. I recognized two of them. We exchanged nods, and I laid her on the table.

Kathryn gripped my little finger firmly as I hovered beside her. The thought that this could be our last connection tormented me. A nurse gently led me aside. My contact with Kathryn narrowed down to her tenuous grip. Then her tiny fingers slipped away. My heart sank into darkness. A heave of fear reached my throat.

Quickly, a circle closed around her table. Groups of nurses and medical technicians appeared, taking up positions, wheeling in equipment; they executed precise maneuvers, then disappeared. They bore one kind or another of devices, syringes, tubing with sharp insertion wedges, trays of glistening stainless steel, wiring and clips, blood pressure patches, charts. A large plastic canopy came down over Kathryn's head. The staff asked me gently again to step back, but I could manage only a few paces. Something far down in my core was being pulled apart. I kept eye contact with Kathryn, despite my tears. My field of view narrowed. Nothing else in the world mattered. Her head was turned toward me, even as the canopy came to rest on the table, covering the upper part of her body. Doctors moved in groups of two and three. The table was now completely surrounded with medical people.

The chief physician began an incision just below her belly button to get fluids and nourishment into her. A nurse motioned me to a chair at the edge of the room. I looked back at Kathryn, now unconscious from sedatives and shock. She had turned a purplish color. I could only get glimpses between the whitegowned bodies and arms. I sat, numb and terrified.

The medical staff began a series of coordinated moves. One inserted tubes into her tiny veins in each arm for nourishment and antibiotics. Another inserted a line in her umbilicus. Others placed patches to monitor her heart. Each move picked up the pace, accelerating like a gas turbine at ignition, the quiet whir of a medical machine rising in pitch, integral parts building to a fury.

Later I learned that her five-pound body was mustering all it could to hold off a virus attacking her heart. She had gone into heart failure. The technical name was viral myocarditis. The virus was winning. Her heart had ballooned to the size of a lemon. Seizures showed that the virus was attacking her nervous system. A doctor gave her a one-in-ten chance of surviving the night.

We sat in traumatic stress as the night blurred into morning.

Overnight, Linda and I had shuttled back and forth to the hospital, looking in on her every hour or so. Being there was the only support we could provide.

Though still a newborn and clinging to the edge of life, Kathryn displayed a titanic will to live. Only later did I come to see that a powerful force must have been stirring inside, fighting for her survival.

In the first hours in intensive care, her strength had ebbed away. Tissue destroyed, her little heart was overcome. By the end of the first week, a pediatric cardiologist came over from San Francisco. His father had first identified a virus with similar symptoms in South Africa. Although the medical name is generic, he informed us that this particular virus appeared in clusters of four to six cases, had a preference for the hearts of newborn females, and was usually fatal. Three other cases were reported in Northern California that fall. No common denominator of hospital or clinic was identified. All those patients had died.

I called my parents the next day. Mom made every effort to be supportive and understanding. I could always rely on that. Dad, who had softened a bit with the arrival of grandchildren, nonetheless seemed distant. I couldn't read him. He projected a kind of moodiness, a bit aloof, as if he didn't know how to act. I gave up trying to figure it out. Both my parents were eager to come to Berkeley from Sacramento to support us and Kathryn.

"Yes, come," I said, "but wait a few days. Just until she is out of the woods."

SURVIVAL AND DEATH

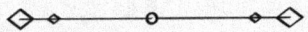

Mom and Dad reached the hospital a few days later. A cloak of shock hung around me 24/7. Linda and I ran on autopilot for the routine parts of the day. We switched into alert mode only in pediatric intensive care. That's where we greeted Mom and Dad.

Their presence was heartening, yet I felt that I needed to show I was in charge. I wanted to show that I could somehow manage this crisis. I couldn't. I felt utterly helpless, like a small animal trapped. They entered a reception room where Linda and I sat poring over medical notes. Mom was warm and supportive, Dad stiff and gaunt. They were eager for news and seemed to feel as lost as we were. Of course, they had even less information than we did.

The four of us embraced. My words were clipped, dry, and uncertain. Dad put on a calm and reassuring air. I couldn't tell whether his was a blind conviction, or a lack of understanding of the gravity of Kathryn's condition. I didn't know how to handle Dad. He seemed genuinely ready to help, but neither of us knew how he could.

They visited her small table in the intensive care ward. The wires and feeding tubes sprouted from a half-dozen spots on her underweight body. They stood with us for a few minutes. I felt as though we were perched either at an altar or the edge of a grave, pouring our emotional energy into our tiny baby. Then my dad took her little hand and gave it a squeeze.

"She will be all right," my father said. "She is strong."

Intellectually, I dismissed his assurances as the hopeful wishes of the loving grandfather that down deep somewhere he wanted to be. But the act itself gave Kathryn and me a small infusion of life energy.

The next day, Kathryn's condition became more complicated. Blood chemistry data, taken every hour to manage the balance of fluids and blood pressure, was contradictory and confusing. Kathryn's intravenous tubes kept pulling free; her small body mass allowed little margin for error. Even experienced nurses had trouble finding her veins and coaxing a minuscule needle into them. She would flinch with each insertion—arms, legs, even forehead. Invariably the lines would have to be removed because the vein had been missed. Witnessing this was torture, an unavoidable concomitant of our support. There was no turning away.

Meanwhile, Alana was abandoned by one parent at a time as Linda and I alternated our visits to the pediatric intensive care ward. The fatherhood project—my inventing a way to be a father that was part dreamy lullaby and part spiritual partner with a rule book and a wink—was now in tatters. My brief times with Alana, fitted in between visits and consultations at the hospital, proved the unraveling. We tried to stay upbeat around her, but inevitably there were fewer trips to the park, and pushes in the swing lost their zest. I put on a brave face for her, and she gleefully met my eyes. But inside we both knew that our play had lost its magic.

At the hospital, the physicians described blossoming complications. Kathryn had suffered an absence of oxygen to her brain, a condition called anoxia, during the initial stages of the illness. The degree of brain damage was difficult to assess, but her frequent seizures signaled trouble. In addition, X-rays showed that her right kidney had decreased in size, possibly due to a blockage of blood flow on that side of her body. And there was the ongoing threat of further heart trouble.

About the second week of her hospitalization, the heart monitor flashed erratically, on again, off again. The beat line made jagged spikes and plunging troughs. Each change jerked us along, our spirits riding on electro-technical beats. The attending physician, one of the cardiologists, called us to his office. We braced ourselves for the news we had been dreading.

"She may not get through this night, and I feel you should know and be prepared," he said. "When the time comes, if you wish, we can turn off the machinery, unplug her, and you can hold her and be with her to say goodbye." He motioned to a door. It led to special room just off the main ward where we could have our last moments with Kathryn in peace. Linda and I tightened our grip on each other. I could not look at the door.

Linda and I were coming up to the summit of the compact we had made for ourselves and for Kathryn a few days earlier.

"We both know that she might not make it," Linda had said.

We sat alone in an empty visitor room facing a choice we dreaded most. Our eyes locked on one another. The deep creases in Linda's face reflected my own anxiety. Her eyes were wet. Her lip folded out as she began to cry, her hands trembling. Then, summoning courage, she drew herself more erect. The trembling stopped. Her eyes bore deep into mine. I already knew where she was headed, but I was shrinking inside in a futile attempt to escape the reality. But the only light was forward, to push back against these feelings of doom and double down on our baby.

"We have to give her everything. Everything we've got as long as she's alive," she said.

"Yes. Every single ounce of love we have, we must give. We must give it now."

"Yes," she whispered. "Yes. Everything."

We hugged each other and wept. We felt certain of our pledge. We had reached into the very depths of our being, where soul and identity unite, and refused despair, gritting our teeth against fear.

Besides the torment of witnessing Kathryn's suffering, we faced overwhelming challenges, whether she survived or not. The deeper our commitment to her, the more acute the loss if she were to die. Yet the medical staff had hinted or said outright that long-term prospects were iffy. We knew that Kathryn's epileptic seizures would likely continue. One kidney was seriously compromised. Heart tissue was scarred. She had suffered brain damage. Some of the medical staff thought that she might never leave a hospital setting, might never escape the dependence of medical-technical supports, might never recover from a vegetative state.

* * *

We stood on a knife's edge. On one side life, with the prospect of unending challenges; on the other, death and an abyss of grief. Either way, we stared into an abyss of emotional debt.

We could have shut down the battle right then and there. Instead, we chose to go all in. We entered a phase of dark suspense, an agonizing watch which gave added weight to each capricious flicker and beep of electronic monitors.

That night melted into morning. A nurse gave Kathryn to me to hold. The dreaded moment never came. If anything, Kathryn seemed to be a little more stable. Her heart activity grew less erratic. We drew a cautious breath.

* * *

A few days later brought new agonies. The attending team wanted to do a biopsy, a procedure to slip a thin wire up the veins in her leg and into her chest cavity to nip a piece of heart tissue for analysis. The doctors had said that the viral attack had scarred the upper left heart ventricle, causing arrhythmias and runs of wild electrical discharges. The proposal for biopsy was presented to us late on Tuesday for a Wednesday morning operation.

The doctor's proposal came as another wave pounding our weakening defenses. No sooner had we beaten back one overwhelming moment—the door I couldn't look at—that another came rolling in. I turned to Linda. She was staring at the cardiologist, her mouth was slightly ajar. I was staggering inside but buoyed by the commitment we had made. We had doubled down on Kathryn, blind maybe to the long-term consequences, but at least not just passively reacting.

The confidence of our utter commitment to her pushed me to speak up.

"What difference will it make?" I asked flatly.

The cardiologist and other medical staff stared back in silence.

"What findings would change her treatment?" I continued. Linda gripped my hand. "What findings would enable you to change the outcome?"

After a pause, the cardiologist confessed, "Nothing we would find would change what we are doing." The team members glanced at each other. Then the pediatrician said, "But we could learn more about what's going on. We're not entirely sure about the virus. Something else could be driving this."

The physicians were earnest—and puzzled by the tortuous path of Kathryn's illness. Was it really a viral infection in her heart or was her heart condition caused by something else, a thrombosis or a congenital defect? They were sympathetic, but their attitude was clinical.

"We can't give our consent," I said, drawing on pure instinct, fighting off my doubts. The physicians stared back, as though unaccustomed to resistance. The cardiologist drew in a breath and nodded, showing he understood our position. He turned and left.

It was not easy to stand against the momentum gathered by the team of pediatric heart specialists. Still, our decision proved correct. The following day, Wednesday afternoon, without warning, Kathryn went into heart failure for the second time. She would not have survived a biopsy that morning.

Somehow, Linda managed her research and clinical work on a skeletal schedule while I effectively suspended my consulting in international urban development. For several weeks, Linda and I settled into a rhythm, marked by a numb determination to get through the day, to attend to Kathryn at the intensive care battlefront at every opportunity, and to maintain a semblance of stability for Alana.

Being physically close to Kathryn took on new importance for us. She was effectively in a coma, on a respirator, and pumped with drugs. Nonetheless, we felt it was therapy for her, however impalpable, for us to orbit silently around her, exerting our gravity on her, letting her gravity pull us in. We would split shifts during the day, one of us driving Alana to day care, the other picking her up, and alternating our time with Kathryn. I spent the nights sitting at Kathryn's bedside and sleeping on a couch in a nearby visitors' room. Linda was at home with Alana.

At the hospital, our hopes were tethered to the dancing, beeping heart monitor. The hourly news of her blood chemistry samples was a continual reminder of her delicate state:

electrolytes too high, with pressure too low, or vice versa. Yet, in time, we came to take each bit of news with muted feelings, not assigning too much hope or desperation to upturns or downturns, as if we had fallen under a prolonged dose of emotional Novocain.

Kathryn was heavily laden with fluids and medications—to control seizures, regulate blood pressure, and steady heartbeats—and she was never conscious. We sat for long hours at her bedside, murmuring made-up songs. One afternoon, I bought a tiny rubber elephant and folded it gently into her gripping fingers.

Her involuntary movements gave the appearance of waving the elephant about: my little baby doing little baby things. I wept.

Intermittently, I would shuttle back to the house to pick up the most important medicine Kathryn would ever receive: Linda's breast milk. Linda continued to express at home. It was not easy, but she did not give up. Her breasts were sore and nipples raw from the breast pumps. Though we were both emotionally battered and depressed, Linda grew stronger and more determined with each week.

I would take the few ounces of milk in small bottles as though I was engaged in a global pharma enterprise. I placed the priceless elixir in a cooler next to me in the car. I carried it carefully into the hospital and placed the bottles gently between Kathryn's lips. Though she was never fully awake, sometimes the aroma would work its way into her system, and she would suckle instinctively. This cheered me immensely. It proved that we weren't impotent. Apart from the elixir, we were there on pure instinct, to be in her psychic field, in her aura, to observe the surface of things, to sing and coo to her, watching for any sign of emergence from her deep stupor.

Kathryn looked scrawny, tiny, pale, near death. A heart monitor was attached to her chest, an IV in her head, a tube in her umbilicus, electrodes and IVs in every limb. A catheter drained her spleen. A black respirator mask covered her face. She wore a knitted hat. I sat on a stool next to her and stroked her head, holding her hand.

Linda adapted the words from a lullaby we often sang to Alana at bedtime during the idyllic phase of parenthood, now in the distant past. The lullaby went like this:

Hey, hey, Kathryn Ariel.
Hey, hey, Kathryn Ariel.
Everybody loves Kathryn Ariel.
She's the special one.

Like a mantra for keeping her alive, we would repeat this over and over. I pretended that the sound of my voice drowned out the monitors and the crying of babies nearby and that she could hear me, even though she could show no outward sign.

When nurses came to attend Kathryn as I was singing quietly, they glanced at me, smiling faintly, not intruding, but acknowledging the therapy that was under way. The nurses knew what was needed. Their tacit support cheered me.

But sooner or later, the monitors and the beeping would get the better of me. Spikes and alarms went off as Kathryn went into spasmodic runs of heartbeats. Tense alarms vibrated in my body; I just had to surrender. My singing trailed off. But I did not give up. I waited for a quiet moment and started again.

* * *

During this period, our friends encircled us. We found meals on our doorstep every night. Friends offered to take Alana on day trips and to drive carpools. These gestures of support cast flickers of light into the darkness of our fear and exhaustion.

Quite aside from Kathryn's dire situation, I felt as if Alana was being abandoned. There is no more stark illustration of this than my utter inability to recall specific moments with her (other than her dance and song) during those weeks. Perhaps my memory loss is a companion to trauma. Linda and I focused on the neediest at any given moment, and Alana inevitably came up second. In those weeks, I felt a tearing in my heart whenever Alana came to mind. Even today, nearly forty years later, I feel the residual heat in my coals of grief. Those moments of separation created a debt to her I still owe, even though Alana herself moved forward a long time ago.

* * *

I hadn't noticed the attending physician as he approached me at Kathryn's bedside. He said, "I'm sorry, it's hospital policy." He gestured to the medical logs in my lap. "I'm afraid you can't be looking at the logs."

I glanced up from my perch on a plastic chair in the corner of the pediatric intensive care ward, Linda beside me. The physician stood over us with a friendly, but firm demeanor.

I had helped myself to the sheaf of medical reports—lab notes and physicians' entries—at the foot of Kathryn's bed. The hospital made a point of welcoming parents and family in pediatric intensive care. We could come and go as we pleased. We talked with the physicians regularly; they were available and open. We felt very grateful to be on the receiving end of that hospital policy. So, I felt comfortable in extending that welcome to the written notes of the physicians. Their qualitative observations accompanied lab reports about blood chemistry, pressures, and temperatures, all of it compiled in Kathryn's binder. The notes only ratified what we were told, but they were blunter.

Words like "difficult night," and "parents are aware of the gravity of the situation" were sprinkled through the pages. There were also many indications—words like "puzzling" and "unsure"—of how much in the dark the medical staff were.

I quietly closed the book and handed it over.

I recognized their liability concerns. I was poring over hard data that might contain evidence that could be used in court. But that was not my intention. Learning about Kathryn's illness, understanding her condition, noting the changes, helped to fortify my confidence and gave me courage to ask questions, to advocate for my daughter.

* * *

Although the heart monitor and the respirator were often the only signs of Kathryn's life, I grew to detest the monitor, even as I clung to its every signal as though all our lives depended on it. That dependency played cruel tricks. Kathryn frequently had arrhythmias. She would show no outward sign of change, but the monitor would suddenly fly into a cacophony of sound and jagged lines and we would stiffen with apprehension, riveted to the screen. The scenes reminded me of submarine movies, boat crews trapped silent and helpless, listening for the pinging of an unseen destroyer overhead. We waited for the awful moment when strings of two, three, or more arrhythmias would appear sequentially, knowing that this spelled trouble—or even the beginning of the end. With a heart rate sometimes over 200 beats per minute and blood pressure over 170, Kathryn's heart was losing its integrity, slipping into a flurry of disorganized contractions. A nurse would push the hard copy button, and a small, inked arm would begin tracing the beat pattern on a roll of recording tape, until she tore it off and hurried away.

The respirator was easier to take. At least it created the illusion that Kathryn had a strong healthy heave to her breathing. Her tiny chest cavity would swell up with each breath. It made her look robust. I was in such a state that even this mechanical contrivance could be translated into hope. But the mask detracted from the illusion. Kathryn was so small; the mask nearly covered her face.

The mask also evoked a ghastly memory. A respirator on Linda's father at the time of his death some five years before had the same effect. He had suffered a storm of heart attacks but was holding on when we arrived at his bedside. His chest was heaving. His tanned body, exposed at the rib cage, appeared like a weightlifter's, drawing in great volumes of air. It took me several minutes to fully appreciate the mechanical imperative of the respirator and the most visible sign of it, the mask. Barney died while we were at his bedside, taking all this in. The image stayed with me. Now the same black rubber mask was fitted over my baby's tiny face.

* * *

A nurse awakened me quietly at four thirty on a morning of the fourth week. Kathryn was going into convulsions. This nurse was the epitome of a health care professional. She'd told me from the beginning that she never gave up on Kathryn. When the trouble started up again, she came to the couch where I was sleeping.

"I think you should come," she said quietly in the darkness. "Kathryn's beginning to seize." Her eyes were focused into mine, letting the message sink in. She was worried about Kathryn surviving the night.

We both knew the tiny tremors in Kathryn's limbs were a sign that her body was losing the battle. I sat next to my baby and held her quivering little fingers. I gave all I could to her, inwardly opening my spiritual core, exposing the innermost strength of my being and projecting it onto her, as though I were hurling a magical cape of immortality upon her. It is a feeling that lies behind a deep grunt, the sound you would make trying to move a mountain, except I was silent. It was not mass that I was trying to move. It was an invisible force, a silent exertion, showing strength, showing defiance, showing tenderness and caring, cradling my baby in my arms. I heard nothing; I had blocked out the chirping electronic monitors. I started a line or two of the lullaby, humming softly, delicately grasping her fingers, the miniature petals reaching out, exposed. I felt quite certain that these were her last moments on earth. But, by God, I was there. I defied lightning to strike—take me if you want—but I wasn't going to let that virus kill my baby, not if I could help it. The nurse would not have noticed this. I sat calmly at Kathryn's bedside, a little bit of Buddha hiding the storm inside.

After a few hours at her side, I felt completely wrung out. I had no tears left. Sometime before sunup, Kathryn fell back into quiet. Miraculously, the dangerous moment seemed to have passed once again. The nurse looked up to me, astonished, shaking her head in disbelief. I felt utterly depleted inside.

Kathryn was showing me something new: a powerful drive to live came from deep within her. She was fighting a titanic battle. Yes, the tangles of technological monitoring and an armory of medications supported her, but Kathryn herself, sustained by her mother's breast milk and our physical presence, won through to daylight.

* * *

I drove home completely spent, yet buoyed by the miracle of Kathryn's survival.

I reached my door sweaty, messy, held erect mostly by will. The phone was ringing as I unlocked the front door. It was a Saturday. Linda and Alana were still asleep. My mother was on the line. I could tell from her pause, her breathing, that the news was bad.

"Your father died last night of a heart attack."

I felt the odd sensation of being the butt of a cosmic joke. At the same time, the shock and timing of Dad's death sent me into an unfamiliar mental state—somewhere in the mixed twilight of grief and awe. The wrenching loss came right at the moment, indeed according to Dad's autopsy, within an hour, of Kathryn's survival from her third heart failure. In the wee hours of that morning, as I was sitting on a stool holding Kathryn's quivering fingers, Dad was lying on the floor a hundred miles away in Sacramento, his heart convulsed in crisis, coming to a shuddering stop.

* * *

Despite the roughness of my relationship with Dad, and because of my understanding of the rocky ground that shaped his life, it was hard not to see how his passing came with a handoff of life energy. The juxtaposition could not have been starker: one life just beginning to emerge, delicate, tender, innocent, and another hardened by the rough weather of age and instinctively defensive. Yet, down under the many layers of emotional rock in Dad was a warm, soft core. He had said that she was strong and that she would be all right.

Standing in my house with the phone in my hand, the front door still open, I envisioned the spheres of my life revolving into a new configuration. Mom would need help, Alana would need support, I was about to ascend to a new station in the family. It was a time to add reflection and preparation to my state of trauma.

PART II

LOOKING BACK: ORIGINS OF MAN TO FATHERHOOD

BECOMING TIM

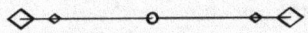

The funeral, held in Sacramento, was a bleak concoction of emotional outpouring—mourning for Dad; consolation for Mom, my brother, and myself; and a flood of stories and memories about Dad's life. Many who attended had knowledge about Kathryn and asked about Linda and Alana, who had stayed in Berkeley to be near Kathryn. Aside from the respectful mourning for Dad, being close to Mom and my brother, Kent, was a welcome, if transitory, relief from our loss and from the bleak, hospital-filled days.

After services, stories of Dad's life began to trickle out from the many aunts and uncles. That's when my aunt Vera told me about the fire of 1919. Her narrative triggered a profusion of anecdotes about Dad's life. Most notable for me were those about him living at the edge of survival growing up with six brothers and two sisters and no father in the household.

* * *

Wiped out by the fire, my grandfather found work far away in the timberlands of Northern California and Oregon.

His family struggled to get by without him. They succeeded thanks to my grandmother's wits and tireless work in the fields and canneries of Gridley. My grandmother drew on deep ties to the Mormon community. Somehow, she found ways to keep the family from starving. Aunts and uncles and friends helped by taking in one or another of Dad's siblings, one on a dairy farm here, another in the orchard farm there. Dad spent several years with a Mormon family in the community.

He and his brothers worked as field laborers from their adolescence through high school. His sisters worked in fruit canneries. Dad's father occasionally sent money and rarely returned home. I guess that's when the layers of his protective shell began to pile up. The absence of his own father and uncertainty about his future molded an outlook of caution, a hardened view of life, and a rough exterior. And although he transmited the values of hard work to his two boys, he also harbored a resentment about the easier life we had compared to his.

Dad did well enough in school to gain admission to Utah State. Perhaps the Mormon connections in Gridley helped to bring college into his life. But though an amazing achievement, his days were lean. To start college, his only transportation across the 700 miles from Gridley to Logan was by freight train. My brother and I heard his tales many times.

Dad hid out in the Union Pacific switchyards in nearby Roseville, evading security guards, called bulls, who were armed with billy clubs. Their job was to keep freeloaders like him from riding the rails. He got a tip from one of hobos waiting in the yards for the right train. My father was fit and well-built, not tall like half of his brothers, but strong. He could take care of himself. Dad found an empty boxcar filled with straw.

He found other stowaways huddled at the far end of the car. The wintry ride out of Roseville wound up the foothills of the Sierra Nevadas. The cold grew more intense as the train reached Auburn and became frigid as they reached the snowline near Colfax.

One guy drew the attention and displeasure of the others. Perhaps the fuss was the result of an old grudge, an unpaid loan, a broken promise. Not long afterward, the fussing brewed into a fight. The train drew near the sheds in the thin mountain air at Donner Pass. The cars passed into and out of long wooden sheds built on the steep slopes to keep snow slides from blocking the tracks. Dad saw a small group set upon the bindlestiff and force him out the gaping side door into the frigid night and down the plunging banks of snow.

Dad started college in the middle of the Depression at Utah State and landed a job in a field station of the department of animal husbandry. It gave him lodging, but not much more. During one friged winter, Dad scoured the cornfields for discarded cobs, gathered them in a bag, and hauled his harvest back to his bunkroom. He boiled the corn for Christmas dinner.

* * *

Dad worked his way through school and graduated a few years before World War II started. He landed a job with the

Farmers Home Administration and when the war began, he was deferred from military service, until near the end of the war, when he was called up by the Marines. His experience in the Marines must have matched his thirst for order and predictability. After the War, Dad returned to the FHA and dedicated his professional life to helping small farmers in Northern California and Nevada, for instance by making loans and offering technical assistance.

Dad sprinkled Marine lore into our childhood—reminding us that he had to make his bunk so a quarter would bounce off it. He would say in a gruff way, "be sure to 'police up,' your room," and things like: "Recruits stay tough, they don't buckle." The message was, you suck it up, remain steadfast in every detail. That kind of discipline seemed to appeal to my father, and he did a good job of imbuing it in my brother and me when we were kids.

"Squeeze the trigger slowly with your whole hand," he would say during our shooting lessons. "Hold your breath the last few seconds before firing." When we went on hikes, he reminded us of basic training principles like keeping your feet pointing straight ahead, not to the side, and to trim our toenails straight across. "Up and at 'em" was often the seven a.m. wake-up call we would get on Saturday mornings.

* * *

At the time we started grade school, we lived on two acres on the edge of Sacramento with a horse or two, a dozen chickens, a few cows, and some pigs. Perhaps Dad sought to recreate his own past in order to master the outcome. Whatever his worldview, he seemed determined to instill in my brother and me values of hard work and discipline. We were taught to do regular chores, like gather eggs, feed the few head of cattle we had, chase down pigs when they made a jail break, and police up the yard. We were made cognizant of the struggles he'd had to endure.

The summer I was six, my father sent my brother and me to stay with our three cousins in Yuba City and work in the prune orchards. The experience was part summer camp, part hard work. We were on our knees all day, picking up prunes alongside families of Braceros, more commonly known as migrant farm workers, who labored in the next row. One day, I harvested more fruit than my next older cousin. His father, my uncle, reprimanded him for letting his younger cousin do more than he did. The next day, I slowed my pace so as to not get my cousin in trouble. That experience opened my eyes in many ways. Besides finding a balance between competitiveness and family ties, I was moved by the plight of Bracero children. They scampered around their parents, who labored and sweated in the hot valley sun harvesting the fruit. For my brother, my cousins, and me, the job provided pocket money, but for the Braceros, it was a livelihood.

* * *

The year following my prune-picking summer, I showed an interest in learning to ride our horse. I thought I was going to get into a saddle, but the lesson turned into a wild adventure. My dad lifted me up like a light pack saddle onto the broad back of our chestnut, Nelly. My legs stuck straight out across Nelly's broad beam like toothpicks in a potato. She seemed impossibly wide and far off the ground. Sitting on top of Nelly was like sitting on the three-room chicken coop behind our house: my view improved greatly. But the chicken coop would never move.

When Nelly shifted her weight, I experienced the first uncontrolled movement of a large mammal beneath me. My little frame swayed with Nelly's every small motion—an ominous shift for me filled with unimaginable potential, yet little more than a sigh for her.

My dad wore a T-shirt and fisherman's cap. He calmly looped a thick cotton rope around Nelly's muzzle, tied a single half hitch on the left, and handed me the trailing end. It was just long enough for me to hold in both hands. I sat with bare necessities: no bit, a one-sided halter, no saddle.

"You can have a saddle when you learn to ride," he said.

I sat dumbly, awaiting further instruction. The sun beat down through the cottonwoods overhead. The heat drove cottonwoody gasses and scintillas into the summer sky. They floated over Nelly's mane and drifted far down the sloping green pasture, over the water standpipe a hundred yards away, on toward the black walnut trees, dissolving off into the squat valley oaks beyond the fence and the creek, a quarter mile down the sloping pasture.

"Indian children grip with their legs and steer with the horse's mane," my dad intoned. This imparted little comfort since my legs were in no position to grip anything. I grasped the rope halter more tightly.

"How do I make her go?" I asked, partly hoping, I remember, that maybe there was no way to make her go without a bit, proper halter, reins, and a saddle.

Dad smiled up at me from under his cap. He said nothing as he walked slowly along the wood fence next to Nelly. He stepped up on the lowermost boards and tore a small branch from a cottonwood tree. He stripped away a few of the off-shooting stalks until the limber main stem, now naked, fanned out with smaller stems toward the end, some with peripheral leaves still attached.

He returned to my side and handed up the switch. "Here," he said, "use this." I took the switch. "Don't hit her hard, and remember, whatever happens, you're the boss."

I was scarcely able to fathom the meaning of these words, feeling more like Piglet, at the small, confused, bottom end of things, than confident Christopher Robin. I felt even less certain about the meaning of the words that followed: "Never let the horse think it is in control. You're in charge, no matter what."

I brought the switch down on Nelly's rump.

She shot into a gallop, heading straight for the far corner of the pasture. The dynamic of her pounding hooves and throbbing muscles boiled up into a calamitous roar. My heart pounded in a similar rhythm. My legs bobbed wildly, my vision blurred, my head even out of sync with my mouth, teeth clattering, the rope halter completely forgotten, my fingers locked tightly around fistfuls of mane. We crashed down the pasture slope for long minutes, my mind at the edge of terror, my body unable to find a pattern in the chaos of movement.

In a blink, there came a cessation of sound, a momentary lull, save for the rushing of wind passing about my ears. In an instant, we had shifted from mad, headlong pounding into a windy, soaring arc. Nelly made a gigantic leap into the air. My position on her became impossible to reckon. I could not be certain she was still beneath me. Sound resumed once again. With a mighty thump, Nelly's hooves dug deeply into the soft, muddy turf.

Even as we approached landing, my nose dove into her mane. My lips, chin, cheeks, and neck slid in a rough caress along her spine, down her neck, and across the broad, warm swelling of her withers. As she pitched forward and planted her front hooves, I slid down her left foreleg like a fire pole and miraculously hit the ground feet first. Coming to a near standstill, stunned and open-mouthed, I stood in shock, halter rope still in hand.

Nelly must have felt the sudden tug on her muzzle as I came to earth, and she drew up the forward motion of her hindquarters and reared to a halt. The whites of her eyes arched high around her dark brown irises as she searched to understand the force being exerted upon her. She bent her head down and around to face me, as if to examine what sort of small thing—this small human boy—had engineered this control after all the calamity. Though shocked by this test-piloting, I realized—standing there at the foot of the water standpipe that she and I had just jumped—that I was still in charge, at least from her point of view.

I reminisced about all of this after Dad's funeral. Yes, I had stuck the landing, even though the landing wasn't the main objective. I did feel some modicum of accomplishment, but I had little appetite to mount up again. More important, small seeds had taken root with the Nelly experience. Besides a sense of achievement—or maybe I should call it a feeling of having survived—I began to feel bristly shoots of wariness about my dad.

* * *

During most weeks of the year, Dad traveled by car around Northern California and Nevada, driving up and down back highways, visiting orchard and vegetable growers for the Farmers Home Administration. He was gone all week. Mom became the sole day-to-day caretaker. She grew into a protective role, offering us a sweet and nurturing presence throughout our childhood. When Dad would return from his long circuits motoring around the state, he arrived fatigued, and often, his mood was dark. He affected an air of aloofness, but his snippiness betrayed an angry interior. If he discovered that we had not finished a chore we were told to complete before his leaving, Dad's anger would sometimes erupt and he would bark at my brother and me. Dad could run slivers of fear through our hearts when it came to hard work and punishment.

When we were really bad—like the time we tracked mud through my uncle's house—my Dad pulled out his belt and whipped our butts. On other occasions when we went astray, he would put on a stern face and cower us with statements like, "Well maybe I'll have to pull out my belt." My brother and I learned later that Mom disapproved. She would calm him down out of our earshot, but we never knew for sure if the belt threat was an empty one or not.

When I was about ten, my father returned from one of his long road trips. He was in a foul mood and growled at us for not completing our chores, like hoeing weeds, watering the vegetable garden, and cutting grass. Mom had gone to the grocery store. My brother, Kent, then thirteen, stood up to Dad in his first tentative gesture of adolescent defiance. My brother not only threw out an excuse, but he also raised his voice and shouted back. Dad's anger flashed from hot to incandescent. He heaved up his barrel chest. The volume in his voice went up by leaps. He was shouting at my brother, who continued to resist. My dad grabbed my brother by the arm and yanked him around. Kent struggled to pull free. I was cowering in the corner, terrified. I cried out for the violence to stop.

My father threw a glance at me as he held my brother's arm with one hand. He seemed to catch himself, and retreated, leaving us in a small heap, bawling. His anger and aggression were frightening, and for years I felt as though we had to tiptoe around and, yes, be sure to do our chores.

When I joined a Christian social club in high school, Dad called me a party boy (he was partly right) and sometimes wisecracked that I was "soft and a candy-ass," by which he meant somewhat spoiled, not up to doing hard work. Though he mellowed in his later years, his resentment toward my soft life simmered well into my adult years.

Of course, in our elementary and high school years there were many days of pleasant outings, even warm family experiences. We camped at Tahoe, picnicked and swam in the Sacramento River, and water-skied at Folsom Lake. One favorite outing was the annual California State Fair. Dad loved to walk us through the county building, a large pavilion where each of the state's counties displayed their agricultural and industrial products. The smell of fresh peaches and floral bouquets hung in the air along with Dad's expert narrative as we toured the pavilion. But these were rare punctuations in the long text of childhood.

* * *

When I was fifteen, Dad's anger came out in another, more sinister way. He sat fuming in the driveway as his Chrysler coughed and sputtered. He had to drop me off at a friend's house and was already running late for a meeting. The car was relatively new, yet as he cranked it over, it failed to catch. I sat on the passenger side of the front seat. He grew more agitated and impatient. I could see the figurative jets of steam blowing out of his ears. Jumping out of the car, he hurried into the garage and brought back a red, five-gallon can of gasoline, with the spout sticking out like a long snake.

"Try some gasoline directly into the carburetor while I turn it over," he said. "Go ahead, don't be afraid, just pour it in there." He wasn't encouraging. He was a Marine, giving orders.

I was afraid. Gasoline directly into the carburetor? Even at fifteen that didn't sound like a good idea to me. I stuck my head under the hood. I felt like I was entering the mouth of doom.

"Go ahead," he insisted. "Just do it," the "just do it" part laden with "don't be a sissy."

I tipped the can and as Dad cranked the engine, a stream of gasoline flowed directly into the carburetor. Immediately, a giant gash of flame erupted upwards, reaching for the spout. My heart leapt with fear. I could feel the heat blast past my face and smelled the combusted gas. It stirred the pit of my stomach. I flung the can back and away. Only a miracle saved me from holding an exploding bomb. Dad saw the ball of fire. For several moments, we were both paralyzed in shock.

I felt a toxic mixture of anger that Dad would put me in that position. I thought he should have shown remorse, apologized, or expressed how badly he felt. He did nothing. My father avoided eye contact for the rest of the day. Eventually, the car started and Dad drove me to my destination with barely a word. We sat in a long silence and entered a willing forgetfulness. I didn't even dare to speak out. We buried it. But the scars from that incident didn't go away easily. The experience capped years of having to skirt carefully around Dad, the volcano. An uneasy wariness built up inside me. I grew ever more convinced that strategic care was needed in dealing with him.

I would have to find an independent way forward, a path that would allow me to set up my own guardrails, to quietly strike out on my own in matters of life and relationships, to be free from the fearful retribution I saw simmering in my father. I felt sure that hidden behind statements like "candy-ass" and "you don't know what hard work is" lurked a deep resentment about how easy my life was in comparison to his own. I knew he was right, and at the same time, knew that part of him really wanted my life to be easier than his.

Many misunderstandings had crowded out the small shoots of trust that might have taken root between Dad and me were it not for the belt, the angry rough edges, and his skeptical outlook on life. It became convenient—less likely to elicit trouble—to simply not ask for his help. It was better to not stand out too much, to avoid confrontation, retreat if necessary, take a precautionary tact around Dad. That strategy also meant not to excel in sports or social life, not to call attention to my success. Getting good grades was OK as long as I was quiet and not showy. But I felt I had to tone down social life and bottle up any successes in athletics. I was afraid that my natural gifts— the witty, loquacious, athletic happy-go-lucky kid—reminded Dad of the things he didn't have.

My strategy got me through high school where small steps in the classroom and social life began to lead me to greater self-confidence. I started college at UC Davis, got pretty good grades, joined a fraternity, and played JV baseball as a freshman. A visit to Berkeley by President Kennedy in 1962 lit a flare of interest for me in the rapidly changing social and political environment that was building around that campus in the early sixties. After three semesters at Davis, I transferred to Berkeley to join that dazzling, expansive world. I saw myself building a separate identity from Dad.

* * *

At Berkeley, I witnessed the political ground shaking under my feet. Each reverberation reinforced the conviction that big social and political problems—like racial discrimination, the growing war in Vietnam, and looming environmental issues—could be addressed, even solved. Daily demonstrations and sometimes police incursions were captured nightly on national news. In Berkeley, you realized that you had to pick up the pace on your walk through life and reach a trot, and soon you were still falling behind and needed to shift from a trot to a run to keep up with fast-moving events.

Late in the spring of 1964, the professor of our political science class of less than thirty students announced that a special guest would be appearing that day. We immediately recognized Kennedy's brother-in-law. Shriver had dark wavy hair and wore a blue blazer and gray slacks, his shirt open at the top. He stood calmly through a brief introduction. The professor sat down, and Shriver stepped forward with an earnest expression on his face. He had our attention even before he greeted us. He spoke briefly about the great social and political divides in the world, a subject that threaded through our political science classes on comparative government and land reform in Latin America. Then he mentioned Kennedy's new initiative, the Peace Corps.

"Join the Peace Corps," he said with firm conviction. He stepped forward, closing the distance between us. He came near my seat, making eye contact with me. I sat transfixed. He looked directly into my eyes. "Join the Peace Corps," he repeated. He pointed at me with his finger like Uncle Sam points in the recruitment poster for the military. "You, you can make a difference in the world." I sat speechless, completely captivated by the idea. For one thing, his message contrasted sharply with the messages I got from my dad. Shriver was encouraging me to venture out and take risks. For another, behind his appeal blew the winds of change we were already feeling on campus.

* * *

I joined and was assigned to a rural land-reform colony in Costa Rica. Peace Corps seemed a perfect segue from my studies at Cal. My job as a community organizer was to identify and help meet the "felt needs" of a couple hundred colonists taking part in a land reform program in a remote rural village. "Felt needs" meant things like water connections, all-weather roads, health services, and school improvements. The colonists' job, besides eking out a living, was to improve their plots as a condition of land title they hoped to gain. Most families nurtured coffee trees on the verdant hillsides and tended gardens and sometimes livestock.

The village center consisted of a small tienda (store), a school, and a bus stop, surrounded by a dozen or so dwellings. Roads little more than dirt tracks branched out in three directions, penetrating the rolling hills and fertile green mountains where most of the colonists lived.

* * *

Within a few months, I was to harvest one of Dad's lessons on self-control and animal control. My job required mobility to visit peasants up and down the valley to understand their problems. Pajaro, a horse rented from a neighbor, was the answer. Getting Pajaro to do my bidding, even getting her out of the pasture, was like a cat ordering a greyhound to play with yarn. For the first time since my wild ride with Nelly at age six, I got back in the saddle and was soon to discover something shocking.

I was returning from a visit to a peasant family one afternoon when Pajaro, tethered to bushes, abruptly pulled free and trotted up the road. I found myself staring at her, the two of us standing motionless, like sweating statues in the hot tropical sun. My saddle sat naked in a mocking perch upon her back.

From her return stare I could see we had reached an impasse. Pajaro seemed to sense that the gringo, who didn't look like any other human she had ever seen, was a little green at this business of horsemanship. Yet, she knew her avenues of escape were cut off by steep slopes, a swiftly moving stream, and barbed-wire fences playing over the foothills. Her only recourse was to head back down the rock-strewn road past me. If I lost that standoff, Pajaro wouldn't be so easily bridled next time I needed her for traveling the countryside. What's worse, she would confirm the suspicions of the campesinos (locals) whose trust I had to earn.

Pajaro would have been delighted to be liberated and get back to grazing. I had learned in my first months of volunteering that chasing Pajaro was futile. Only the sweet guayabas that lay strewn about a lone tree in my yard could bring her in. But on the road that day, I had no guayabas.

As I held her gaze, I remembered the earliest days of learning horsemanship from Dad—of riding bareback, of animal control and self-control. Dad's words flowed into my mind: "You're in charge, no matter what."

Pajaro eyed me, seeming to measure my resolve.

She lurched toward me, nose thrust forward. She hit a gallop in two strides. Stirrups flapped like the broken wings of some tropical Pegasus. Rocks rolled and flew in all directions.

My muscles stiffened; my mind jangled in a calliope of images and sounds. My mouth felt like dust as all the moisture in my body seemed to flow to my brow and armpits. Pajaro sped straight toward me, the whites of her eyes gaining intention, her ears laid back. The thundering in my head rang louder than her hooves.

Above this clamor, a wisp of memory emerged of my childself striking Nelly with the cottonwood switch given to me by my father. Nelly had shot out from a standstill under the cottonwood, a steel pinball rocketing faster than the speed of squeal up a narrow shoot with the same spontaneous burst of energy Pajaro was now discharging toward me.

Pajaro's silhouette shifted from barrel chest and reaching forelegs to speeding freight train. Her dark mane and tail flew. Her broad body and clattering hooves pushed dust and gravel into an upwelling tidal wave about to break over me.

My teeth clenched. My heart flopped like a netted fish. In split seconds, my resolve firmed up, melted away, then renewed. I harbored a small hope that Pajaro might, at the last instant, break to one side. But this was balanced by the fear that she might just as easily make me part of the road.

My life clearly hung on the edge of a tossed coin: either Dad was right about animal control, or I would be trampled into gravel and dust.

A force inside me jutted out my arms, stiff and wooden, like a cross, but I could not close my eyes. My father's words echoed once more in my head: "... no matter what." I looked unflinching into Pajaro's rushing form. Our eyes locked. Her ears popped up signalling a change of heart. I tightened my fists. She was within a few yards, and the moment had arrived. There seemed a moment of silence.

Pajaro's forelegs stiffened, her hooves plowed into the gravel, dust billowed forward. Her rear hooves bit into the road; her head flew up and out at a tortured angle. In sputtering confusion, within two strides, short stepping, nearly hopping, she came to a standstill. Her momentum carried her rear end around, her body now nearly broadside to me. The reins swung forward, still playing out the forward motion of her wild break for freedom.

Like Nelly, twenty years earlier, the whites of Pajaro's eyes arched high. She bent her head down and around to face me, as if to examine this astonishing gringo.

Dad had been proven correct, a big payoff for a tough lesson. I mounted Pajaro and rode her back to the corral, tipping my hat to villagers here and there. That experience launched a new phase in my life, not just as a Peace Corps volunteer, but as a person—a man who in a few short years would become a father. I felt a fresh breeze of confidence that I'd rarely felt around Dad.

The Phantom Captain Appears

One night several months later, after a small gathering of fellow volunteers and local friends in the capital, San Jose, my date and I warmed to a mutual attraction. Incidental contact at the party, even in the permissive personal space of Latin culture, evolved to gentle brushing—shoulders at first, then breast on shoulder, and full-on leaning into one another at the drinks table. "We can't go home," she whispered. "My parents are there." My small hostel offered no privacy either. Without a suitable place to land, we wandered the streets of the neighborhood, hand in hand.

We drifted into shadowy corners, our desires about to spill out into the open. At last, we found an unlit wall along the sidewalk, and I pulled her close to me. She came willingly and pressed hard against my body. I lifted her flowing dress and made a small tent. Vertical sex in the public domain increased the intensity of the moment. We hovered together in the darkness for nearly an hour, maneuvering by feel, until at last we leaned gently against the wall, murmuring away the afterglow.

Later, I walked her home, then made my way along a residential block toward my hostel. In the middle of the block, I caught sight of a large dog ahead and across the street, slinking in the opposite direction. Having already had many unpleasant encounters at night with canine strays, I kept a careful eye on my unwanted company as the distance closed between us. We passed each other, eyes warily in contact from across the narrow street. After we passed each other, he then crossed to my side, still heading away. At ten yards, he swept through the scent of woman still lingering in my trail.

At that moment, I turned to check his progress and saw him react as he met the scent. He drew abruptly to a halt and jerked around. The stray stiffened and bared his fangs. He laid back his ears. The fur on his neck was standing like jackstraws, the furrows over his snout and forehead were deeply knotted. His eyes were in a fearsome glare. He leapt forward half the distance between us with a frightening, ugly growl. I was petrified. No help around, nowhere to run.

In an instant, two animals emitted deep feral eruptions in the street, each answering the other. I felt as though my veins shattered, the hair on my scrotum stood erect. For long seconds, the shocking surge of oral fireworks came shooting out from deep within me. The loudest and most dominant guttural snarling was coming out of my throat. I was shocked at the tightening around my neck, the awkward angle of my jaw, the force of the air being squeezed through my windpipes, most of all, stupidly aware, but completely unable to affect, the noise and intensity of my primitive vocal outpouring. It built to a jet-like roar streaming through my mouth. My shoulders were tense, muscles and hands rigid. I could barely breathe and felt as though my airways were clogged, my body sprung tight, like the poor mutt that challenged me.

The dog blinked. His fur lay down; he drew back and looked away. As quickly as he had gone on the offensive, he turned and trotted away down the street. It took me much longer to recover. I was stunned and motionless for long minutes, reabsorbing the animal in me.

"What the hell was *that?*" I muttered into the quiet night, my limbs trembling.

To my rhetorical question, the Phantom Captain, a survival force in me, in my dad, in all of us, might well have answered. "You were in danger. It's my job."

I was twenty-three and had just turned into an animal. I had trouble weaving that traumatic moment into the fabric of the person I thought I was. I saw myself as pacifistic and non-confrontational. I steered clear from Dad when he got hot. In high school, I walked away from fights. After college, when Vietnam was raging, it was the Peace Corps I joined, not the war corps. Over the years, the encounter with the dog bit into my consciousness. That was when it dawned on me, that earlier moments of crisis shared a common feature.

The Phantom might have been around during the gasoline bomb incident and the stampeding horse in Costa Rica. I realized that at that moment, an invisible force intervened. When I was a toddler, something saved me from drowning (I only remember seeing the bubbles against the swimming pool wall). As a teenager, I awoke abruptly sitting at the steering wheel of my speeding truck heading straight for a tree on the roadside. A force—was it the Phantom?—had acted in my life at many dangerous moments. I decided to call the force, the Phantom Captain. Phantom, because he's ghost-like. He comes and goes without warning. And Captain, because when he does appear, he takes charge to save me, as he did with my dad, the dog, the oncoming collision with a tree.

I often mused about the Phantom, seeing him as my little pet savior evolved in our limbic system over evolutionary time. With the passing of years, the Phantom faded from view. A decade later, after Kathryn was born, he would return, and my view of him changed drastically.

INVENTING FATHERHOOD

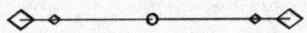

After Peace Corps, while getting my doctorate in Cambridge, Massachusetts, I met Linda, a New York City girl. It was a warm evening in 1973. I wandered into the university square and saw her sitting with her friend at a small restaurant. We connected at first sight, each of us brightening when our eyes met.

Later that night, lounging in her apartment, we lit a fire and talked about ourselves and our dreams until the wee hours of the morning. She had a PhD by the age of twenty-four, was an established professional, as well as smart and beautiful. Taking a break from hours of talking, Linda strode into the kitchen to put on water for tea. As she reentered the room, I asked her if she ever thought about having children. Without breaking stride, she raised her arm high in the air with fingers crossed. A wannabe mother. I was hooked.

A month or so later, while enjoying the beach, we shared our still-forming dreams about having children. Linda had strong training and nearly a decade of experience as a professional psychologist. She knew a great deal about children. The beach was filled with families. A small child caught our attention. The toddler wanted to run off on his own. The father playfully positioned himself as a barrier, turning control into a game. Both were laughing. "That's how you do it," Linda said.

The scene struck me as a counterpoint to the gruff, strict control I got from my own father. I became even more convinced that Linda was the woman I wanted as the mother of my children.

My sister-in-law, a talented designer, created our wedding rings from the gold of our mothers' engagement rings. Our matched set featured small, concentric arcs, like a rainbow, springing from atop a circle, representing the sun. Adjacent to the sun was a smaller circle, a moon in our orbit. The moon represented our offspring. Our first moon came along several years later.

* * *

With the birth of Alana, I was determined to create my own version of a father. I aimed to be a soft, accessible teddy, but with authority and a wink. All the dreamy visions I had imagined seemed within reach. I wanted to be able to put myself in my children's shoes, but also to keep my perspective, to remember the quaking moments my father engendered when he was threatening, so I wouldn't be like that. I wanted to be approachable, someone they could trust, someone more like my mother. They would understand and accept my authority because they identified with me and I with them, not because I was a strong authoritarian.

I would be the protector, though. I wanted to see far

ahead and keep the big world clear of menace. I would not just clear the forest of tigers, but also forge a path for opportunity. I'd create a space for my children to be nurtured and to grow. Goal defined, I quietly set about engineering a style of fatherhood that fit my personality.

Of course, I ran into many small bumps in the road. When it came time to change the first diaper, Linda and I puzzled over the instructions on the disposable diapers and laughed at ourselves. Forty-eight years of formal education between us and we couldn't figure out how to tape that damn diaper.

For most of Alana's infancy, Linda and I jostled to be the first at the crib to pick her up and hold her. Giggles, playful jousting, and endless staring at Alana filled her early years. She was everything we had dreamed about. Linda was the perfect mother, deploying her natural, nurturing instincts. Alana reciprocated. Our family bond deepened by the day.

As a father, I came to realize, I had a comparative advantage in some things and was utterly useless in others. I made a swinging bed out of a hanging basket chair and suspended it from the ceiling at the foot of our bed. We would lie quietly in the afternoons, nudging the swinging bed with a foot while Alana drifted off to sleep.

But dads aren't even in the running at the most critical moments of infant life, like nursing. Observe any mother nursing. That scene made it patently obvious that dads are at a sharp disadvantage in bonding. Yes, we can hold the bottle, but the look of utter bliss on Alana's face, locked onto her mother's eyes as she nursed, is not something that dads can experience. On occasion, I had a not-so-secret desire to bond with her the same way. I once offered her my own nipple as an experiment. Alana yawned and looked away.

I did get good at cooing and putting on diapers. I loved the return gaze as I sang softly and caressed my little one. Not quite as good as nursing, but close. We had the then-cloth diapers in piles, and I was proud of being able to achieve a tight wrap quickly and comfortably, safety pins and all. On occasion, I had inspiration with dressing her as well. Simple tops and diapers were about all I could handle—not too many colors or patterns to match. The urge to be a stay-at-home dad grew, even as I continued working for local organizations and firms as a consultant in international urban development.

Day by day, week by week, I delighted to see Alana expand into her world—with her understanding, her mental comprehension, her language and vocabulary. I was in awe of the human being unfolding before my eyes. I guided her, and she taught me. The pace was brisk.

By the time she turned two, she began to take part in the plan for the day. On one bright summer morning, she exclaimed, "Oh no, that wasn't my plan!"

"You don't want to play with the button box?"

"No, Daddy. I want to stir the pancake mix."

I slid the button box back in the cabinet with a grin and carried Alana into the kitchen.

"OK, then, pancakes it is." I was the new dad, learning the ropes.

Linda was just getting started on a research project at her

workplace in San Francisco. I struggled to manage my free-lance consulting while finishing my doctoral dissertation. Our little house on Oxford Street in North Berkeley was modest, but plenty comfy for the three of us.

When Linda began to work more regularly in San Francisco, I would do the daddy commute, packing Alana into our little car and ferrying her over the Bay Bridge for a nursing lunch. That could get tough when hunger pangs showed up early or when Linda was running late. One long afternoon when Alana's meal was way too late, she gorged and then slept, and facing mounting traffic on the commute back home, I parked at the curb in front of a bar that featured Monday Night Football. Alana was fast asleep in her car seat. The 49ers were playing some team back east, so I watched the game through the bar window while listening to the play-by-play on the radio. I saw myself living the good father life, finding a way to enjoy the mobile man-cave and still be with my daughter.

In the late 1970s, many parents in our circle spoke about sexism. Waves of political and cultural change washed over Berkeley during the decade before Alana was born. Move-ments for women's equality, along with environmental sensi-tivity and Black power, dominated the news. Young parents were resolute about gender bias. No more guns for boys and dolls for girls. We did our level best with Alana. She received as many trucks, balls, and tennis gear as dolls, skirts, and pre-tend jewelry. We were careful to balance out gender references in language and ordinary conversation. Our efforts to be gender neutral became a natural experiment. It pretty much ended when Alana filled her truck with glittery stuff, put on a tutu, and asked her mom to try lipstick.

When Linda was off to do her psychology work at a hospital in the city, Alana and I spent our days going to the parks, getting frozen yogurt, and playing in the house or the yard. One of her favorites was the slides at Codornices Park. We went shooting down the long winding concrete slide on flattened cardboard boxes. She wanted more and more; her laughter punctuated by ecstatic screams. Then the swings. I loved the swings as much as she did. We would go for hours, me pushing her and making conversation about the other kids, our neighborhood, the wider world. Next stop, off for a snack before naptime.

At night, I would make up stories about a unicorn that rose from the Marin headlands and circled over children's homes in the Bay Area as the sun went down. The unicorn spread magical dust—we called it stardust—that calmed the worries of children and helped them to sleep. To this day, Alana and I talk about stardust not from unicorns, but from the expansion of the universe and the explosion of stars, creating all that we know in our physical world. My life as a stay-at-home dad was sweeter than I had imagined.

Three or four times a year a consulting gig materialized, and the pangs of separation hit hard. One morning when Alana was three, sleeping in her own room, I arose at four a.m. to finish packing for a trip to Africa. I crept around in the dark so as not to disturb Linda. Quietly, like an angelic doe, Alana appeared in the doorway.

"Honey," I whispered. "What are you doing up so early?"

"I came to say goodbye, Daddy." She spoke matter-of-factly.

"I'm amazed you woke up."

"I wanted to see you before you left."

We looked into each other's eyes. My gut turned over. This was a feeling I never experienced with my father. My dreams were coming true. I was being magically transported into a world beyond fatherhood. The worship was mutual, but Alana didn't know that. I walked her back to her room and tucked her in with a kiss and long hug, doing my best to hide my tears.

At the layover at JFK, I phoned Linda. Facing three weeks away from her and Alana was torture. I thought of my father's long absences and worried that I was beginning the same routine he had lived, being pulled away from family, afraid that I was repeating his pattern despite my best intentions. I fell into full-blown bawling. What the hell was I doing going off to Africa? I should be at home. Linda comforted me, but the pain was inescapable. Passengers hurried by and must have wondered what was up with that guy at the pay phone. They might have understood, if they were fathers, that I was a young dad cutting my teeth on separation.

When I returned at last, Linda and Alana met me at the San Francisco airport for a joyous reunion. Linda was radiant and affectionate. Alana's blond hair surrounded her bright eyes. Our hugs were tight and prolonged. In the baggage area, Alana spotted my bag and grabbed the handles with exaggerated glee and tugged at it. The bag weighed more than she did, but she was showing me that she was there to help. That was a welcome home I'll never forget.

Though my work required travel, when I was at home,

I could dive into my role as chief playmate and carpool driver. I relished our time in the little, aging green BMW. One day, I found a plastic replica of a P-51 fighter airplane taped to the hood, like a rakish ornament, a gift from a playful friend, Row-bear. Except this was no ordinary ornament. It had a bright red fuselage, a fifteen-inch wingspan and a spinning propeller. I discovered while driving that the plane had special features. At speed, the tail would want to lift off the deck, straining against the tape. It wanted to fly. The replica was so good, that the camber on the wings produced lift. The car was pretty beat up by that time, so I drilled two small holes in the hood under the landing gear of the plane. Using ordinary coat hanger wire, I shaped two miniature retaining struts, hooking them onto the landing gear and secured them into the holes in the hood. Linda smilingly rolled her eyes.

Alana and her friends loved the plane. The propeller wouldspin in a slow roll. The kids in the backseat craned forward to watch the action. At seventeen miles per hour, the tail would lift, like at takeoff. At thirty-five, the entire plane would lift off the hood and fly. It gave the impression that a flying car was following the plane. We all yelled and whooped and pretended we were flying a plane and not driving a car. Coming to stops at crosswalks, pedestrians would point and rock back their heads with a laugh as the propeller wound down.

A few months later, I bought a used radio that had a tapedeck built in with a microphone on long coiled cord. It stretched to the back seat. We would drive with the plane flying, and Alana and her friends would make pilot chat or sing into the tape deck and play it back as we rode. Alana and her friend Kit sometimes fought over the microphone.

Kit said, "Alana, stop being crabby, or we won't get any treats."

"No, Kit. If we're crabby then we will get treats." She had my number, even then.

At her preschool, I occasionally spent time on the playground.

"OK, everybody. Sit in a circle," I'd say. Alana's toddler-mates gathered around, sitting in a sandbox shaped like a boat.

"We're on a large sailboat, and we're sailing for a far-off island." Giggles and wide eyes looked around.

"OK, everybody, now we're on the beach. Everybody, dig your toes into the sand." A flurry of small toes squiggled into the sand, making a pit.

"All feet in." The toddlers loved to be in the circle, imagining a seafaring activity.

"Deeper, deeper, deeper, everybody." I covered the eighteen feet with mounds of sand. We all giggled.

"OK, snack time. Feet up everybody. Time to wash up and get indoors."

Laughter and uniform enchantment. My idyllic model was working. One night, at a school event for parents, a teacher mentioned to visiting parents that Alana's daddy was just irresistible. I quietly accepted the compliment with pride.

It was less than two months later that Kathryn fell ill and only a month after her hospitalization that my father died. I had no clue that my early plunge into fatherhood had left me completely unprepared for the next appearance of the

Phantom.

PHANTOMS AND FATHERS

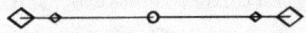

My fatherhood project was now complicated by the imperative of Kathryn's survival. Yes, she'd made it through the night of my father's fatal heart attack, but her charts were filled with unanswered questions about her future. I couldn't be sure she would even survive the hospital, and, if so, that she would emerge from a vegetative state. Doctors had warned us that survivors of childhood viral myocarditis sometimes run into trouble, even die, when the heart becomes overwhelmed with the rapid growth that comes with adolescence. What sort of family life would we have? Almost every conceivable answer to those questions led me far, far away from the image of fatherhood I had dreamed of inventing.

It was no longer a simple matter of creating a fatherhood free of my father's mistakes. That idyllic world with Alana had been obliterated. After the shock of facing what I'd feared were Kathryn's last moments, I couldn't see how it would be possible to restore that thrill of creative bonding, that exalted role of godlike dad.

At Kathryn's bedside in the hospital, I felt pulled down into a defensive crouch, like a sentry on the lookout for the smallest threat—a cough from a stranger nearby or a cool draft in the room. I began to see my dad in me. I feared that I was drifting toward my dad's pattern of fathering, one that was dominated by fearfulness, constant defensiveness, even paranoia. What would it be life for Alana to grow up under a father like that? Being on guard to meet the real and imagined threats to Kathryn was driving a stake right through the heart of my vow to be a different kind of dad.

That night, trying to sleep at the hospital, I lay awake, eyes wide open in anxiety. I thought of the Phantom Captain and saw with new eyes my—and my father's—reaction to threats. My mind went back to the confrontation with the growling dog, my paralytic fear of a nearly exploded gasoline can, and my volcanic father.

Could I control the Phantom in me? I put myself back in the scene of erupting flames in Dad's sputtering Chrysler. A hot, pungent odor had filled my nostrils. A bolt of fear had shot through me. I slipped into a hypnagogic state and glimpsed a shadowy image of my avator and imagined a conversation with the Phantom. It might have gone like this:

"No doubt about it," the Phantom would have said. "Your dad's a threat."

"Wait a minute. He's my dad," the younger me would have retorted, plaintively. "Yeah, he was careless, maybe hostile, but he's taken care of me in so many other ways."

"I don't care about that. My job is your welfare."

"What do you mean, *your* job? What about my job, to

take care of myself? That's one of the things my dad taught me."

"Doesn't matter. You could have been toast. I'm keeping an eye on him from now on. You have to be careful too. Besides, it's not the first time I've had to act when your family was around."

"What do you mean?"

"Remember the drowning incident?"

"You mean at Reno, when I was three?"

"Exactly. Grown-ups were all around the pool, but you were going under."

I stared into space, recalling one of my earliest memories. Bubbles and a blue haze filled my field of vision as I sank beneath the surface. A babysitter had lost track of me. I was sinking. Somebody pulled me out.

"As soon as you went under, I slid behind the autonomic dashboard and pulled the levers to slow heartbeat and stop breathing," the Phantom Captain said.

In my mental conversation, I got a wider view of a force inside me—inside my dad, inside all of us—that takes charge at critical times to react to threats. Dad's life was filled with cautious, defensive reactions. Now I could see the force of the Phantom acting on me as well.

Yet, my Phantom intervened and acted without my permission, even without my knowledge. That struck me as irritating. Intrusions into my life without my knowing. What about self-determination? What would that mean for my own fathering?

"Who are you, anyway? Where do you come from?"

"Let's just say I'm your instinct to survive. You know, limbic system, amygdala, hypothalamus . . . all that."

"I guess I should be grateful for this . . . gift," I said. The Phantom shrugged. "Is everybody's phantom like this?"

"Yep. More or less." Then he paused. "I guess it's a little different for females. They have something more. They're inclined, you know, to tend and befriend as well as fight or flee."

I sat puzzled. "What do you mean?"

"You know, women have a different way of dealing with stress. Part of their survival instinct is being good at befriending others and tending to their family. For men, it's mainly fight or flight."

I thought of the higher density neurons in parts of the female amygdala that were thought to be associated with processing and articulating emotions. Women have a "thicker" emotional experience; they can wade into it, examine it, talk about it.

"But I'm troubled, too," I confessed, after a few moments. "Suppose I don't want you to intervene? Why can't I just take care of myself?"

"Doesn't work that way," he replied. "It's on or off for me. When I get the signal, I move. Like with the dog and Pajaro, I either attack, run, freeze, or hide, your survival's at stake. It's my choice. It's an evolutionary thing. Nothing you can do to change that."

"You must be kidding. I can't have you intruding whenever you get anxious about my well-being."

"Sorry, that's the way it is. I don't have any say in the matter. It comes from way back," he said, matter-of-factly. "By the way, it's the same with your dad, only his Phantom worked in overdrive. His Phantom stayed more in control."

"Wait. You can be controlled?"

"Well, not really. I act before you even know it. But you can anticipate my actions. You have a choice about whether to let my automatic defenses pervade your personality."

"Yeah," I said. "You mean like my father never made that choice?"

"Exactly. Your dad never learned to manage his Phantom. Too many things were a threat."

* * *

I saw that I had a larger challenge before me if I wanted to preserve my dream of reinventing fatherhood. Somehow, I had to stay positive, nurture and encourage the best from my children and, most of all, be on the lookout for sudden eruptions of the Phantom when stress or threats reared up.

The path my father had shown me led to the gruff action of bull-rushing aggressively forward, knocking down all opposition as a kind of defense or to hold back and be cautious. He was just like my Phantom. The other path, the one I was hoping to invent, and which was now under a darkening cloud, was the warm protector, the father who could fend off the night with the warm light in my eyes. But lurking around in the dark was the quickness of the Phantom.

The teddy-father seemed like Little League compared to the Phantom. For one thing, I felt the pressures of playing the conventional, stereotypical role of strong, stoic, protector and provider. I could smell the lurking emotional traps. Yes, you can bluster and charge forward. Yes, you can puff out your chest and claim victory. But that's like the Shakespeare line spoken by Glendower in Henry the IV. "I can summon spirits from the deep ocean," to which Hotspur replies, "Why, so can I, and so can any other man! But will they come when you summon them?"

I saw the posturing and bluster of the stereotypical father as an empty salve for the ego. That was my father, badgered into a corner by ill fate. Only in his later years did I appreciate the kind and warm person that was hidden inside. Besides all that, with Kathryn's illness, the stakes had changed.

Skyholder

The very first test of my cherished fatherhood model came at the moment of telling Alana about her grandfather's passing. It was bedtime the day after his death. Alana was already tucked in. Linda and I lay on either side of her, giving her warm hugs as she snuggled close. I had a strong image of my father, hovering above me and to the left, looking on as I searched for the right words. Linda and I were numb from the torturous hospital routine. I felt as if a towering wave was building impossibly high over my head and was about to break over my tender little girl. I tightened with stress and worried that I couldn't stay steady.

"Honey, I have some bad news," I started. Immediately, I stumbled internally over my poor choice of words. She drew her head back, seeming to prepare for the gravity of the moment. She pulled her gaze into focus. I waited long seconds, and then said in a low, serious voice:

"Last night, your grandfather died." I tried to make the words plain and flat. How do you tell a bright three-year-old about this, when for months she had been practically abandoned? I sucked in my doubts. I had to be clear and strong, yet I tried to deliver softly.

Alana was silent. She looked down and seemed to collapse a little inside, her expression grave and pensive. There was a flash of sorrow, a hint of shock, a long moment of silence. Wetness formed in her eyes, but she seemed strong, perhaps inured by the emotional hammering she was already taking because of her sister's illness. She was silent, perhaps thinking about riding on grandpa's tractor, or sitting on his lap as he buttered his toast.

Finally, she asked, "Where is he?"

"He's with Grandma and Uncle Kent." She was quiet again, absorbing the idea.

"What does he look like?"

"Honey, I think he looks like he always looked with you, tender and loving."

"What about his teeth?" she continued, searching for some way to make the new reality concrete. "Does he still have his teeth?"

"Yes, sweetheart, he still has his teeth. They are still there, like always."

Alana then placed her hand under my chin, pulling up my face to have a more direct view, sensing that I too had eyes much more than moist.

If I passed the test, it wasn't by much. She was comforting me. I felt like my insides were wrung out.

The wave was cresting. How was I to hold back the tsunami of grief and fear and still be that playful guide I had been practicing in Alana's first three years? I had to provide stability amid the chaos, a shelter from the storm of random crises. Yet there I was, already playing catch-up, attempting to calm the skies after two thunderclaps in a row.

I was in a twilight zone of fatherhood. My model of fathering—close contact, playfulness, and exchanging the lessons of love, language, and life—wasn't going to cut it. Now there was a decidedly grimmer, more practical, more clinical role to play. The vow Linda and I had made at Kathryn's bedside now stretched out of the hospital and into the horizon. We could glimpse our lives being pinched off by the need to protect Kathryn. I had to have steady, resolute strength. I had to persuade my little girl that she was safe, even as her world shuddered from another blow of a capricious fate.

I pictured myself standing over Alana with my arms extended upward. I had a new, overriding mission: to hold up the sky for Alana and Kathryn, to keep it steady in place, benign and predictable. I had to be the skyholder.

Knowing I didn't want to be like Dad was the easy part. But in the days after Kathryn's survival and my father's death, I was realizing that my knee-jerk reaction to threats was essentially the same as the one that had guided Dad for most of his life. I feared that the automatic intrusions of the Phantom Captain would cut into my free will to decide how and when to be defensive and how to be the father I hoped to be.

I needed to stave off my own, Phantom-induced instincts, or at least turn down the volume enough to provide a stable, harmonious life for my disabled child and her gifted sister.

I realized also that I would have to integrate a little more of the feminine side of the Phantom, to summon up the "tend and befriend" instincts—to see issues from the kids' point of view, to develop strategies to reduce stress and solve problems. I had to expand my fatherly repertoire beyond the fight or flight. I hoped by being cognizant of the deep-seated Phantom drive to be able to avoid the coarser parts of the cave-man response. I didn't need to cede my manly will completely; I would be a more effective man, willing and able to react to threats more like women do.

I had to look for ways to integrate different shades of softness into the idea of manhood. I promised myself to look for refinements, to invent a hybrid model. No hulk could punch Kathryn's virus in the nose. But also, no soft Teddy Daddy could save my daughter from dying. I would not settle for that binary choice. There must be many shades of fatherhood. I was on the search for the shade that fit me.

PART III

LOOKING FORWARD

A NEW NORMAL

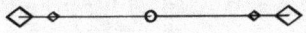

In the weeks following my father's death, Kathryn inched forward. The fluctuations in her vital signs and chemistry grew less frequent. She seemed to be drawing strength from some unseen source. A little color returned to her cheeks. Gradually, by ounces, her weight crept up. Her powerful will to live was beating back the virus. While in the ICU, she had dropped nearly a halfpound below her birthweight. Two months later in October of 1981, weighing over six pounds, she was discharged to our care. Our spirits were lifted, but the grim and demanding hospital routine only shifted locales.

After months in the hospital, we had entered a stressful world of foggy anxiety. I felt as though my fatherhood role was now being played out on a dark and windy pitch, never sure which way the ball was going to roll. Linda and I slept fitfully, interrupted by the routine of giving medications and by the trauma of the experience still stirring within us. As our home became a clinic, we had frequent memories of fear and stress we had felt at the hospital. Linda and I plodded along on the edge of sleepless uncertainty. We were told that any simple infection could have been fatal to Kathryn. We had to administer multiple medications every two hours around the clock. But she was home—tiny, vulnerable, and alive.

Oddly, I felt that the foggy anxiety, our PTSD symptoms, were helpful in some ways. They kept us focused inward, attentive to Kathryn and Alana. Our friends offered to help. We appreciated their offerings—for instance, meals left on our doorstep and offers to stop by—but we were not disposed to respond. We couldn't bridge the gap between their normal lives and our turbulent fear and anxiety. Our inward focus was helpful in fighting off dark clouds of despair, but we paid a price in sleep deprivation, never sure whether the quiet from her crib was a sign of danger. Regularly, we would check her fingernail tips and lips. We studied her fingertips for the telltale pinkness and to see whether color returned after a gentle pinch. That told us that her blood flow to her extremities was healthy. Our automatic nervous reactions—much like the Phantom lurking nearby in physical threats—kept us attentive for any sign of danger.

* * *

In the months following her return home, we found time to finish the official record of her birth. That gave us the opportunity to capture her essence with a name change. We had given a lot of thought to Alana's name. It had a root in both Gaelic and Hebrew, meaning strong-willed fighter and branches of a tree, respectively. It was a perfect fit for Alana. Before Kathryn's birth, we had settled on "Catherine," after a grandmother on each side of the family. Because of her battle, we kept the name, but changed the spelling. Her fight had been so titanic, she had fought so valiantly. Somewhere we saw a reference to the name—spelled Kathryn—in connection with "strong-willed fighter." We changed her middle name from Ann to Ariel, meaning "light and fairy like." It seemed a fitting tribute to her fragility and strength. It still does.

* * *

One of the lowest moments during this period occurred in late fall. I came upon Linda alone in the living room. Her expression evoked a deep hollowness of despair.

"I can't do this," she said quietly. Her eyes were reddened from an hour of weeping. She had been crouched in desperation after finding Alana, who had been left with Kathryn for less than a minute, lying next to Kathryn with her nose in Kathryn's mouth. Alana was acting out a toddler's gesture of affection. To Linda, the scene represented a threat of life-and-death proportions.

"How could she do this?" Linda asked quietly. "I told her that Kathryn mustn't catch a cold." She stared at the floor. "Kathryn could die of a simple infection." A pause filled the air like a dark fog. A shudder went through me.

Linda looked up at me, her face twisted as if a dagger had just been plunged into her heart. She shook her head.

"I can't believe it." Linda was near a breaking point, but she did not crack. She carried many burdens, keeping her career going, bringing in the lion's share of income, even as her infant was on thin ice. I quietly comforted Linda and later gathered up Alana for some one-on-one time to create some sense of normalcy. But there was nothing normal about our lives.

For more than a year, we administered medicines to Kathryn. Various liquids and pills were dosed out round the clock. Digoxin and phenobarbital made us the most anxious. Digoxin was to strengthen her heartbeat, but it also could be complicated, causing kidney problems and electrolyte issues. Phenobarbital was prescribed to ward off seizures, yet the proper dosage for an infant as tiny as Kathryn was a worry.

Phenobarb (our shorthand term) produced a flurry of effects including excitability and irritability, which made it especially hard to get Kathryn to sleep. We were in a crash course on the impacts of medications and the interactions of drugs. Medical personnel assured us about dosages and contraindications, but the wild course of her disease left us wary and raw. We were fearful about the drug's impact on her mental development. We knew that it might have the effect of throwing a wet blanket over her sensibilities, possibly affecting her learning. Concerns about long-term effects cropped up continually.

It seemed that Kathryn would be active and alert, only to turn into a floppy doll, dull and listless for hours after the medication. She had already been through so much medical intervention. Seizures were scary and unpleasant, but the doctors did not make a compelling case about their dangers. In the early eighties, one study showed little evidence about the long-term adverse effects of seizures. Eventually, after consultation with our medical team, we decided to stop phenobarbital. Seizures might come back, but we felt that continuing the meds would risk stunting other areas of growth. We slowly reduced her dosage over months, finally weaned her off the drug, and crossed our fingers.

Late in her first year, Kathryn would often appear out of energy, her eyes vacant. She would stare at us, struggling to comprehend the complicated things going on around her. She was slow to pick up cues. She would look at a book and turn the pages, but not really seem to see the picture of a child with a puppy on the page. Also, her core musculature was weak, and even with support could stand only unsteadily. She began to hold herself sitting upright at eight months and started walking weakly at fifteen.

"It's due to her insult," the occupational therapist would say. (The term "insult" was used often by medical people to refer to the impact of a disease.) "Her corporal resources are overtaxed. It will take time, but she will gain back muscle tone."

That wasn't all there was to the story. Kathryn also suffered from *petit mal* seizures, brief episodes that would flit through her brain and after a few minutes pass on. During those moments, she would stare blankly, in a kind of brain brownout.

Unsurprisingly, Kathryn's developmental milestones appeared late. Her first words like "mama" and "dada" were uttered at about eighteen months. At the same time, Kathryn was an extremely cute child and frequently attracted remarks of admiration from strangers.

The simple act of eating brought another surprise. As she outgrew the bottle, we started Kathryn on solids, an important milestone. But as we fed her, we watched in confusion as Kathryn chewed her food, but didn't swallow. We thought she didn't realize that you swallow your food after you chew it. Kathryn chewed slowly and stared at us. Language was of no help. What does "swallow" mean to a child who hasn't learned to talk, much less to swallow? She took another bite, but her cheeks only puffed up fatter. She chewed and chewed.

"Here sweetie," I offered with wide eyes and a spoon full of mush to capture her attention. She looked at the spoon, made a few more chewing motions, then looked at me.

"Here, watch Daddy." I put another spoonful in my mouth and chewed. Then, craning my head upward and pointing to my throat, I made a swallowing motion. Kathryn stared at me, her chewing suspended. She looked at Linda, standing next to her. Our coaxing drew a blank. Try showing and telling somebody how to swallow. It's not in any daddy's book of rules. For most of us, the action is instinctive. She looked like a tiny chipmunk, cheeks all puffed out with food, a puzzled stare her only reaction to our futile gestures. I think she got little bits of nutrition by osmosis, but in the end, the mouthful would get ejected onto her high chair tray.

It took us some time to realize that her musculature around her mouth and throat had been affected by the trauma of her illness, just as her larger body muscles were delayed in development. We already knew the virus had left her heart stiff and less pliable. The rest of her body also didn't develop as in normal kids. There was no remedy for the failure to swallow other than to give her more liquid food. Eventually, her musculature improved, and one day, many weeks later, she swallowed all on her own.

At about this time, Kathryn started both occupational and speech therapy, and she found her own ways to make up for her deficits, even before she knew they were deficits. When she was three, she took immediately to a tape recorder to play songs and recorded stories. The tape recorder was fire-engine red, plastic, nearly the size of a waffle iron, and had a little handle on one end. She carried it around like a miniature suitcase, grasping a clutch of tapes in her other hand. The tape recorder was her favorite transition to sleep for naps and bedtime. We would sit with her and and Alana, taking turns reading stories until they drifted off to sleep. Kathryn didn't go easily. "Again, read it again," she would say. Eventually, we read into the tape recorder, and she could listen over and over as I dozed by her bedside.

One day with Kathryn at the local swimming pool, I saw her drift off to sleep on the pool deck, her little butt to the sky, head down, resting on the tape recorder. She wore bright red sunglasses that matched the tape recorder, a miniature bikini—white with red piping—a gift I had brought back from Brazil. Little red flip flops lay about her feet.

Occupational therapy aimed to improve her muscle tone. The therapist would sit on the floor, facing Kathryn, who was lying on her back. Holding Kathryn's hands, the therapist would pull her forward, then let her gently back, working to exercise her core muscles. They did a half dozen other kinds of exercises, for back, upper legs, tummy, arms. Kathryn tolerated the routine well enough, but sometimes showed confusion about what was expected of her.

She wasn't the only one confused. What was expected of me? I felt lost about how to handle these unexpected tasks, like swallowing and physical therapy. Help came from my brother Kent in the form of visits and emotional support and from my mom once she emerged from her grieving. But Kent had his own family, and both he and Mom lived a hundred miles away. They were limited in what they could do. My strategy was to keep my eyes open, my sensitivities on high-gain, and my readiness at full alert.

* * *

Meeting Kathryn's many requirements was a heavy load. The time-consuming labor diverted attention from Alana. For her, routine moments that should have been quiet teaching and bonding time could easily get pushed too far. We acted out an unconscious drive to overcompensate, to push Alana academically to make up for Kathryn's deficits. We put extra emphasis on small things in school, finishing homework to a "T" or adding some extra flourish to an assignment. Sometimes Alana would react, sensing the pressure was a little too much.

Miniature power struggles between Linda and me would ensue.

Alana was sitting at the top of the stairs. Her eyes were red. A curled lip and chin pushed out in a defiance. Her mother stood over her, glaring down.

"Alana, I told you to finish coloring in the art project."

"I did," she replied with a huff.

"You haven't colored the parts you are supposed to color."

"I don't want to."

Linda was insisting that her daughter complete an elaborate arabesque in colors. Alana was only four. The project

94

called for filling in many small details. The task was a bit of a stretch for Alana.

The tension boiled over. Alana was at her limits, squirming and beginning to cry. Linda was not backing down.

"You are not getting dessert tonight unless you finish the story."

I was lost. How do I break into a scene after the forces had already been unleashed?

"Linda, don't you think it's a bit much?"

"Don't get into this." She snapped at me.

"She's only four."

"I'm handling this." Another glare.

"But you're over the top."

"Don't undercut me." Her eyes drilled into me.

A fatherhood moment was upon me. Those questions of where to draw the line for my child and for my wife were smack up against me again. Linda was in a protracted PTSD, pushing Alana to exceed. Alana was already struggling just to hold on to her world. Was it better to step in somehow, to shield Alana, or inherit blowback from my intervention and risk escalating the conflict? Or should I just bail out? And then where would I be as a protective father in Alana's eyes?

I decided to leave it there. Let Alana know there was a division. I retreated down the stairs, hoping Linda would lighten up.

It was the first of many times Linda and I clashed over how hard to push, how much discipline to impose. None of the lessons from my dad were of any help. Finding the balance for myself, my child, and my wife, were in my lap. We found ourselves in a recurring loop. I would overreact to my own father's unempathetic discipline-setting by being too permissive. Linda would be holding a steady line, sometimes in the pursuit of normalcy. For the entirety of five years, we were operating in a foggy uncertainty, trying to act like normal parents even though we were still grappling with a child who had to struggle mightily just to remain a part of the living world. Linda was determined to maintain goals like family development, mothering, and education. She was playing out her best parental instinct; I was playing out mine. She wanted to repair the damage from our tragedy by pure force of will, aiming to act as though things were normal. But they were not normal. Her reserves were not up to the task. Neither were mine. We drifted as partners, our relationship on autopilot. The sense of mutual loving sank under the weight of minute-by-minute home care.

* * *

It wasn't all dark. Kathryn began to develop a sense of herself distinct from others, a kind of proto-independence. She could dimly perceive that Alana was something more than a big sister, she was also a caretaker. But that responsibility didn't always sit well with Alana, and occasionally it led to tensions. Something inside of Kathryn, a hidden defensive mechanism coupled with raw determination, showed itself.

When Alana was seven, she decided to challenge Kathryn, perhaps because Alana was tired of her little sister's incessant demand for attention coupled with her blossoming good looks.

"Kathryn," Alana asked, "what's three plus three?"

Kathryn, then four, stared at her sister, her expression

blank except for a small mental whirring that could be perceived in her eyes. She could barely perceive that the challenge was about arithmetic but was completely unable to fathom the calculation. Kathryn prolonged her stare and then, after a minute or two, as her sister produced a vague smirk, Kathryn defiantly blurted out what sounded like "stammish."

"Stammish?" Alana said. "What does that mean?"

Those of us standing around were equally puzzled, but a little amused by Kathryn's defiant gesture. She found a way to rise to the occasion, making up a word.

"Yes, Kathryn, what does stammish mean?" I asked.

Then Kathryn replied. "Stammish. You know. Shit." She paused. Then, "Stammish." Our laughter, including Alana's, filled the room. Kathryn beamed.

* * *

The charming independence developing in Kathryn helped to lighten our load as parents. But there were many more conflicts than moments of mirth.

After some battles, I would stand in front of the mirror asking myself "Where in the rule book is this? What became of the solemn pact that Linda and I pledged in Kathryn's intensive care ward about giving everything, giving all our love?" That beautiful moment had been inundated over time with the flood of medications, the requirements of the working world, the need to manage one recovering child and another who was feeling abandoned. I felt continually pelted with questions about my independence as a father, about balancing softness and taking a hard line. I wasn't up to the female style of exploring and verbalizing emotional stuff the Phantom talked about. In moments of conflict, I thought I was failing. But I was wrong.

RIVETS UNDER THE BRIDGE

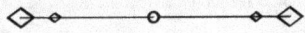

The day-to-day demands of care for Kathryn crowded out attention I had given so lavishly to Alana in her first years of life. The fatherhood role obliged me to be like Janus, the two-faced Roman deity. One face toward Kathryn looked to the careful ministrations of medications, monitoring of color, temperature, and pulse, and scheduling time for her physical and speech therapy.

The other face looked in the opposite direction to attend to Alana, who needed another kind of loving care. She was bombarded by demands no one her age should have to cope with—a dying baby sister, the death of her grandfather—all in a few months. Worse still, Linda and I frequently had to leave Alana with friends to visit medical specialists or get lab work done for Kathryn. Bright and articulate, Alana seemed to absorb the emotional beating she was taking, but signs of stress soon popped up.

One afternoon, Linda and I found time to dedicate to Alana. Relishing our presence, Alana began to dance. We were her audience seated on the sofa, giving her our undivided attention at last. She strode into the room, proud and upbeat in her favorite raspberry-colored leotard. She twirled, arms out at her side, her head cocked back, dancing a made-up dance. She spun around in lazy circles and began to sing. The first and only line in her song sent my heart through the floor.

"My beautiful world is falling apart," she sang. She turned repeatedly around the room, singing with a bright smile on her face with no apparent recognition of the gravity of her words.

"My beautiful world is falling apart."

Several weeks later, Linda found Alana playing a hopping game in her bedroom. Alana explained she was hopping from island to island because, she said, "There are crocodiles in the water between the islands." Linda read the signs and arranged for Alana to see a child psychiatrist. She described him as a "talking doctor."

Seeing a shrink at the age of four was unusual in those days. To my father, it would've been unthinkable. I'd seen a psychologist twenty years earlier after graduate school to help me manage turbulent emotions after returning from the Peace Corps. Dad looked askance. He had asked, "What good will it do?"

Alana's talking doctor lived in Sausalito, a forty-five minute drive from Berkeley, and the biweekly trip offered an opportunity for Alana and me to escape the drumbeat of medicines, labs, and hospital visits for her sick sister. We eagerly sought to rediscover the magic that Alana and I had invented on playgrounds, at the beach, and during picnics in her first years before Kathryn. On her visits to the "talking doctor," we would piggyback an outing together.

The wheels made a crunching sound as they rolled over the mixed gravel at the house of Dr. S.

"Here we are, honey," I murmured. Alana opened her eyes as if on cue. Her proto-meditation complete after a long drive around the San Francisco Bay, she raised her arms so I could unbuckle and lift her out of the car. I opened the gate into the yard of Dr. S's office. "I'll be right here," I said quietly, following our routine. Without a word, she followed the short path to the sliding door where the talking doctor was waiting.

An hour later she came trotting out, a bit of a bounce in her step; she seemed refreshed. She was ready for our adventure.

"Where shall we go, Daddy?" she asked, her face wide open, eyes like saucers under arching eyebrows. "What did you decide?"

"I have a special place, a secret place, a place we've never been to before," I announced. She looked up with anticipation. "It's a place almost nobody knows about. We are going to the bridge, under the bridge." She beamed as I lifted her into her seat.

"We can go under the bridge?"

"Yes, I know a secret way."

Then, haltingly, I asked, "Did you enjoy your hour with Dr. S?" Part of me wanted a glimpse of where Dr. S was going with Alana. What was he finding out? But I was questioning myself as well. Was this really the direction I wanted to go with her?

"We played with stickers," she said. "I told Dr. S a story with the stick-ons."

"Did you tell him about our afternoon?"

"I didn't know we were going under the bridge," she said.

"Yup, *under!*" I decided to stick with my job of creating something fun and memorable for the two of us.

Alana had been over the Golden Gate many times, and we always loved to poke around the Presidio, explore Fort Point, Land's End, and the beach. But we had never been under the bridge. Somehow, deep inside me, I felt that crawling around the gigantic structure would offer us some solace, a way to see a part of the world that stays in place, that has weathered many storms.

We crossed the Golden Gate from north to south. "Look how *high* we are," I said, pointing off toward the city, far away and down below.

"I can see a ship. There's another one." I could hear her fingers tapping the glass, her voice pitched with awe.

"And just about underneath us right now, way far down, is where we're going to be in a few minutes," I said.

Parking at Fort Point, I found my old passage behind the Fort, a place I had visited often as a graduate student in the 1970s. In those days, (before 9/11), it was possible to scale the steep, grassy slopes and wind one's way to a point directly under the span.

"Let's go straight up here, honey," I beckoned to her, extending my hand as we started up the steep slope. The air was clear and crisp. The wind made our cheeks rosy.

Up we went, holding hands, laughing and giggling, our excitement rising with each step up the grassy hillside. The undercarriage of the bridge dominated our view. Out through the latticework, we could see the afternoon sun shimmering on the Pacific. The steel girders of the huge structure crisscrossed and soared above us. We stood like Lilliputians beneath it.

"Can you see the top, Alana?"

"I can only see the bottom," she said, peering up into the web work of steel painted International Orange.

The cars made muted *whooshes* hundreds of feet above us.

"Look, Daddy," she exclaimed, "a doll." A weathered Raggedy Ann was lying in the grass. "And there's a radio." A small transistor lay battered and forgotten. We poked around at the footings of the great soaring beams. A blanket of urban detritus lay about, undisturbed after a long fall: discarded rivets, car radio antennas, plastic bags, pieces of someone's diary, a woman's address written on a corner of a piece of paper, a lighter, a chunk of molded plastic. A small gathering of trash and treasures had made the same fateful drop from high above, each with a story contained in or about it, waiting patiently to be discovered, perhaps put back together.

"What are these big things, Daddy?" Alana said, pointing at some rivets lying in the grass.

"They are called rivets. They are like nails for steel, and they hold things together, like the bridge."

"Magic holding-together things." She paused. "They must be magic to hold this giant thing," she said waving at the bridge.

Piles of rivets, each nearly an inch thick, some a half-foot long, broken and jagged, lay strewn about the hillside. They were worn and looked as though they deserved a rest after a long life of service. Most were fractured, as if from having been mis-struck. They were heavy, of solid steel, covered with faded, reddish-paint matching the strong hue of the mother bridge.

"Oooh, they are heavy," Alana said, picking one up.

"So right you are, little one. These pegs hold together all those big pieces that go from there to there, up and down, and across," I said pointing up to the crossbeams. The heads of the rivets formed long, even lines and complicated patterns at the intersections of the beams.

Though thick and heavy, they were tiny compared to the girders they fastened, and we marveled at how the million small steel pegs could hold that massive conglomeration of metal above us.

I stared up, blankly. *Where are my rivets? Where do I find rivets to keep my world together?* The seismic waves of Kathryn's illness had stressed the trusses holding up our lives. I could see no way to repair them.

"Can we take some home?" Alana asked. "The holding-together things?"

"The rivets? Great idea," I replied. "Let's pick out three or four of the best. You pick three and I will, too."

We poked around, bending over to sort through the rivets, selecting the ones with the most paint.

"This is like Easter eggs," Alana squealed, as she darted around.

Her ebullience gave me a small lift out of the gray funk that had come with so many hospital hours visiting her sister.

The Bay air was beginning to cool in the late afternoon,

and we made our way back down the hill, many pounds of rivets pulling on my backpack.

At the foot of the hill, we spotted an open gate to Fort Point, a large fort built before the Civil War, now dwarfed and tucked under the bridge that was erected seventy years later. With daylight still left, we clambered up its walls and steps to a small wooden lookout nestled high on the fort wall.

"Your castle, my princess," I exclaimed, with my hand extended toward the sea. Alana beamed and with fresh energy ran up to me on the parapet walkway and threw her arms around my legs, giving them a tight hug.

"I love being under the bridge, Daddy." Her head arched up, eyes glistening with joy.

That's when it hit me. I had taken my four-year-old to a psychiatrist, and here she was giving me therapy. Alana was my magical holding-together thing, a small rivet for me and the family.

"And I love you, sweetheart," I murmured, my arms pulling her close.

Near us, a large window of the lookout lay open, facing west. Solid beams of honey sunlight bathed the surroundings. I sat Alana on the sill, a few rivets in her lap, and snapped a last photo for the day. With the sun setting behind us, we loaded up the Datsun and headed home, a collection of unlikely, reddish-orange treasures nestled in the seat.

ERIC IN THE NEW NORMAL

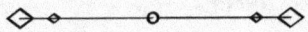

Linda and I had become co-parents, each of us with our nose to the grindstone managing the kids but not nourishing our relationship. Despite our struggles to find a common parenting style, there was one thing Linda and I didn't have to debate: the need to restore the sense of being parents in a normal family. Part of that was planning to have a third child.

By the time she turned two years old, Kathryn had filled out enough to look like a normal baby, and the round-the-clock medications had ended. We knew that barring some bad flu or bacterial infection, she was out of the woods in terms of survival. But her brain anoxia, heart failure, and kidney issues hung like dark clouds over us. We soon learned that she had suffered some hearing loss, as well, and though we faced a certainty that therapies would be needed for a long time—months, if not years—we began to understand the routine. We knew what to expect.

The idea of pushing forward sprang from our sense that Kathryn's illness was an anomaly, that we had been hit by bad luck with unfavorable odds, and that despite the emotional beating we were taking, despite the burden on Alana, things would be better with another, healthy child. Our load would even out with newborn joy in the house. One of our close friends questioned our judgment.

"Are you sure you want to run that risk?" he asked. Linda and I dismissed his concern.

Our dream of normalcy, the bliss that Alana had embodied, drew us forward. I hadn't given up completely on the idyllic model of fathering. I thought that having a new addition—and who knows, maybe even a boy—would resuscitate our vision of parenthood. Linda and I both needed hope for a less grim world.

Financial issues were a more practical concern. Linda's work provided insurance that covered the steepest slopes of our mountain of medical expenses. But her project was coming to an end. Bills piled up from Kathryn's hospital stay as well as from doctors, specialists, therapies, and drugs.

One evening, Linda pointed to a stack of papers more than a foot high. "This is just the first few months," she said dryly. She was stoic, but anxiety tightened her words. "We're getting near the million-dollar mark." That made me swallow a hard, dry swallow, like at night when something goes bump. The bills were so impossibly out of proportion with the realities of our world that we ignored them. We whistled past the debt cemetery, believing somehow insurance or divine intervention would find a way.

"It's my turn," I said, voicing a pledge we both knew to be right. "I'll find a real job, something reliable." I was still freelance consulting. Linda was winding down her clinical research position in San Francisco. She had been carrying the financial load during our acute turn of bad fortune. She was wrapping up her research project, writing articles that would later become a book, seeing patients to augment household income, all the while caring for a desperately ill infant. She felt sharply the financial burden of holding up family finances and didn't want to take on more patients, but felt she had to in order to make ends meet. She needed me to pitch in more.

My international consulting practice, if you can call it that, was a little better than hit-or-miss. Freelance consulting from Berkeley on international poverty and urban development had its challenges. Marketing, traveling, doing the analysis, I joked I was a one-man corporation with five operating divisions. But there was nothing mirthful about the tension around income.

Linda earned significantly more than I did in most years. Painfully aware of the discrepancy, I'd continued to search for assignments, except for a hiatus immediately after Kathryn's hospitalization. Clients were usually large, international organizations—the United Nations, the World Bank, governments, engineering companies. When I did succeed in landing an assignment, behemoth client organizations felt little need to accommodate small fry like me. One Thursday night before a Friday departure for a work assignment in Pakistan worth several months' income, a telegram arrived announcing a cancellation of the mission. Another big, fat bubble in the proverbial income stream.

I had prized the freedom of choice and my independence, but in our new circumstances, my consultant status made me feel helpless. Now my standing as family provider got whittled down with each vague promise of a contract, each uncertain timetable, each cancelled mission. I felt diminished as a man.

As the pressures of caring for Kathryn and Alana grew more intense, I needed to turn up the provider power. I felt ready to take on something new. It wasn't a matter of whether to do it, but how. I was still working to complete my dissertation. I found work at a local energy research institution and small firms in Berkeley.

At Linda's urging, I hired a consultant on employment. I strategized and got more systematic about the search. I looked harder for domestic consulting assignments, so I could stay closer to home and enjoy more reliable scheduling.

* * *

About the same time, late 1984, Linda was nearly ready to deliver Eric. The therapy of a new arrival worked wonders for the whole family. We renewed closeness; we cuddled with Alana, then seven, and Kathryn, three, and wrapped our arms around each other. We could feel ourselves approaching, if not turning, a new corner. Alana had started a very good private elementary school, and Kathryn was speaking in simple sentences. Linda took the lead on shopping for clothes and new things, boy things. A sense of normalcy seeped back in the door.

Then came the naming puzzle.

"We can't name him after a living person," Linda said, explaining her opposition to the name Kent, my brother's name.

"But I'm not Jewish," I countered.

"I am." She winked playfully.

"How about something neutral?"

We quickly abandoned our deep dive into historical and

symbolic meaning for a name. Alana's and Kathryn's names resulted from careful matching of the person with a past or a symbol.

"How about Eric?" she said.

"Sounds great. I like it. How about Eric Kent?"

"Done," she said with a smile.

* * *

Whereas Kathryn had been born so quickly, Eric was a big boy and took his time. Linda was in labor ten hours. She delivered in the alternative birth center at Alta Bates in Berkeley, just as she had with the girls. When Eric finally crowned, the doctor, who was perched on a tilted plastic chair, suddenly inched over a tipping point and went flying backward across the delivery room with a bellowing yell and the crash of the chair hitting the wall.

Startled by the clatter, Linda shrieked: "What happened?" Later, she explained that she was terrified that Eric had popped out onto the floor.

"No, no, honey, it's OK, it's OK." I rushed to help the doctor get to his feet. "Eric's OK. It's just Ron. He fell." Ron got to his feet with a sheepish look on his face.

"What an entrance," he said, smiling. Eric's little angelic forehead had just made its appearance.

We called Eric, Mr. Wonderful, because he was such a contrast to the emotional cacophony of Kathryn's first years. Just what the proverbial doctor had ordered. It seemed our gamble paid off, our reward a beautiful, perfect baby boy. He was placidly agreeable, dreamy, quiet and sweet, and beautiful just like his sisters. In the first months, we would marvel at how different our son was from our expectations. He behaved no differently as a newborn than his sisters, not the chesty brawler that we sometimes saw with our friends' little boys.

One afternoon, changing his diaper, I found myself mildly surprised catching sight of his little man equipment, an appendage instead of folds. As if to punctuate the point, Eric promptly peed high into the air.

Eric offered the opportunity to recapture some of those moments of idyllic fathering, except now we had company. An outing in the park or to the lake became more like we had imagined before Kathryn's illness. She always required a more watchful eye, but ordinary routines of meals and play replicated our earlier experiences with Alana, and Eric's presence put some spring back into our routine.

* * *

One afternoon, when he was past two years old, the phone rang. A woman's voice was filled with anxiety. The manager was calling from Eric's daycare center.

"I think you should come right away." She paused. "Eric seems to be in some distress."

I thought perhaps a scuffle or fight, perhaps some disagreement over toys, but he was barely past two years so it was hard to imagine. On the road, my mouth began to go dry. Memories of driving Kathryn to the emergency room three years earlier were still fresh. The day care attendant met me at the door. Her expression was intense. I began to feel a creeping weariness in my stomach. I looked up to the sky, half thinking thunderclouds were gathering.

"Oh, I'm so glad you're here," she said with evident relief. She turned and led me toward the backyard. We traversed a hallway in the small building, toys arranged in bins, play areas left and right. She called, "He's out here," back over her shoulder to me as she stepped into the yard.

Eric was lying face down on the grass, his arm wrapped around his head. Another attendant squatted nearby, watching over him. I approached quietly and bent down to place my head next to his.

"Eric," I said softly. He remained still. I put my hand on his back to stroke his shoulder. "It's Dad."

When I touched his back, he lifted his head enough to see me over his arm. He rolled halfway over and then started to get up with a flow of tears. I put my arms under his and lifted him to me. He wrapped his legs around my trunk and his arms around my neck. He held on tight, looking pale, sobbing and whimpering. I couldn't get my arms far enough around him. I held Eric, letting him sink into my body, soothing him and stroking his back.

The childcare staff looked on, seemingly paralyzed.

"I wasn't aware of anything specific," one said at last. "He didn't fall. I found him there," she said haltingly. "He was at first unresponsive, then inconsolable."

Eric's sobs began to diminish. I sat down with him in the shade, holding him on my lap, his head cradled in the crook of my arm, his face nestled in my side. I waited for him to calm down, then began speaking softly to him, stroking his arm and his back.

"What is it, big boy? What happened?" He looked up at me without answering. His eyes were sad and confused.

I was perplexed. There was no fight, no fall, nothing traumatic that anyone saw. We drove home in silence. Linda and I discussed the incident. We took him to his pediatrician. She was puzzled too and suggested some testing. Linda worried that something deep was going on. Inside, I fought against the idea that anything serious could be wrong, but, as with Kathryn, I should have watched for clues more carefully.

A week later, we left Eric and Kathryn with a sitter and met with an auditory technician. "I can't believe this," she said, looking at the printout. "Eric has a significant hearing loss." She spoke dryly. Her words were a kick in my stomach.

Hearing loss. We looked at each other, stunned, then embraced. Linda's eyes were as vacant as the yawning pit I felt in my stomach. For the third time in four years, a bolt of lightning had struck: a mysterious malady no one could explain. Our illusion of safety shattered once again.

As before, it was Linda who had first picked up the clues about Eric. Looking back, we began to assemble the details that, in isolation, had not made a complete picture, but in retrospect, fit a pattern. Linda had noticed that his words weren't coming in at the right time. Plus, there were frequent ear infections. Eric was the last one to respond to prompts in his preschool, as when the little ones moved from one play center to another. Eric would be standing at the water table, for instance, when all of his playmates had already moved on to clay or paint. None of those clues by itself set off major alarms. Each could have been explained by something else, like distractions, inattention, or ear infections. But also, we were thrown off track. Kathryn's speech specialist, referring to Eric, had said that it would be too soon to tell whether there was any hearing loss from the infections.

Later testing revealed that Eric's hearing could be augmented with hearing aids, but the loss was permanent. We stared at a twisted irony, feeling as if we'd been snakebit. Someone sent the book *When Bad Things Happen to Good People*. Friends and neighbors closed in as before. The rawness and the emotional demolition were there, but less pronounced. Maybe it's like being a medic in combat. We got inured; we withdrew imperceptibly inside. It was self-preservation.

Yet, I wondered how that saving of emotional energy would play out over time. Would my self-preservation—pulling emotionally inward—make it less likely that I'd have the closeness to him that I had with Alana and Kathryn? I redoubled my resolve to connect to him, my boy. I saw a higher fidelity me in Eric than with the girls.

* * *

As we absorbed the reality of Eric's hearing difficulties, the differences in our parenting styles emerged anew. Once again, my reaction to my father's sandpaper exterior, reinforced by my mindfulness of the Phantom, nudged me toward a softer, easier relationship with the kids. I reacted and sought to protect Eric from his vulnerabilities.

I flashed back to a time of my childhood. One summer morning when I was about ten, my dad found me still in bed at nine in the morning. "Get out of there," he said, barging through my bedroom door. He wasn't yelling, but the gruff tone made it clear that he wasn't about to brook any laziness. Dad was intent on finishing a patio of homemade concrete pavers. "Get out of bed, we've got work to do."

I had a mild flu, but that didn't seem to matter.

Now, as a father of my own son, I felt a reinforced urge to protect Eric.

Linda, on the other hand, had grown up in an environment shaped by a family tragedy of her own. When Linda's mother, Bess, was eight years old, she was the one sent to fetch a doctor for her mother, Linda's grandmother, who had begun having difficulty in labor. By the time Bess had gotten back with the doctor, Linda's grandmother and her newborn baby had died.

Growing up, Linda's mother learned the best strategy in life was to do what needed to be done quickly and without fail, to leave no stone unturned in a task, often ignoring her own emotional needs in a situation. Her mother's struggle with her loss left an indelible mark on her family.

Linda's mother, much like my father, was the dominant figure in her bleak neighborhood of limited resources. Her mother insisted on high standards. Her father, a softie, was more like my mother and didn't take the lead in providing for or protecting the family.

Linda knew at an early age that a good education was the surest escape from her isolation in the difficult neighborhood where she grew up. She was always well organized. As a young child, Linda collected dolls, baseball cards, charms, and other things that she would sort and organize. She earned excellent grades in school. She easily got into college and graduate school.

Linda's mother gave her lots of help. While in graduate school, her mother would sometimes type her papers. At other times, she would go down to the New York City Public Library to check out books that Linda needed. But most of all, she insisted that Linda be responsible and cooperative, that she put in effort and try hard to follow the rules, that she do what people asked her to do.

The stress and threats of uncertain outcomes for Kathryn and Eric made Linda stricter, insisting on the highest standards for all the kids in behavior, chores, and homework. For her, that was the ticket to success, no matter what their initial setbacks. Our goals were the same—high standards for our kids—but her tough love clashed with my softer approach. In homework sessions, for instance, Linda would be more likely to say, "No, that's not right, you have to do it over." I'd more likely say, "Look, if you submit that you will have to live with the consequences."

* * *

Our stress increased as we gradually saw the fallout from Eric's hearing loss. As he developed speaking skills, we saw the telltale signs of incomplete reception. There were no "esses" in plurals, for example, dogs and cats became "dogth" and "cath;" there were no d's or t's in past tense, for instance "didn't" became "didn." He spoke as though his tongue was a little too large for its place. Fortunately, his natural intelligence, dreamy quality, sweetness, and mostly good humor helped him win friends and extra attention from caretakers and, later in school, from teachers.

At the same time, I feared a scar was being formed. It wasn't a physical blemish; his psyche suffered a little bit every day when Eric could see his classmates and teachers couldn't always understand what he was saying. Consequently, Eric became more avoidant, resistant to work because it required so much energy.

Every time I heard his slurred speech or jumbled words, I felt a little dart hit me inside, yet I didn't want to be continually correcting. I remember trying to brave my way through his statements with friends, even his cousins, somehow hoping that with time it would get better. It did in fact, but something else happened also.

It wasn't just hearing and speech clarity. Eric also suffered from auditory processing difficulties, which meant internally, he had to work harder than anybody in the room to make sense of sounds he was hearing. I didn't fully appreciate the mental burden he had to carry and wish now that I would have jumped in more often, to repeat words, watch his eyes for comprehension, perhaps say things he was hearing from others in a different way.

Deep inside, I had hit a wall. The emotional tax we paid every day caring for Kathryn drained my reservoir and made it more difficult to find new energy for Eric. That dilemma didn't present itself as a choice moment to moment. It was more like the acute attentiveness we had been giving Kathryn for four years dulled my perception of Eric's needs—for instance, to study carefully his interactions with the world, to step in when I might have perceived a misunderstanding. My attentiveness had been blunted; more stimulus was required to trigger action.

And unlike the trauma with Kathryn, which was a protracted day-to-day struggle for life, the matter with Eric was over before we knew what was happening. Four years before, Kathryn's illness unfolded hour by hour, minute by minute, with mechanical and electrical rhythm keepers like heart monitors beating out the drama. With Eric, his hearing loss, whatever the cause, happened quietly, insidiously, hidden from view. We were presented one day with a *fait accompli*.

Was there a connection? Were Kathryn's and Eric's hearing loss from a common source, something congenital? We traced back medical and family histories, but without conclusion. No hearing loss was found on either side of the family. We felt helpless.

* * *

I caught sight of Linda nursing Eric. She had nursed Alana in the same way. One day at the playground, I found Linda on her back in the sand, her arms over her head. Alana stood with her feet in the sand, her body leaning over Linda's chest as she nursed. The scene cheered me. I watched approvingly then as I did when she would cuddle Eric and coo to him as he lay in her lap. Her breastfeeding Eric worked magic for everybody. Like a defiant time out, we entered a miniature sanctuary where Linda threw back the debris of trauma in our lives. Her mothering gave Eric and me moments of calm and hope. Eric nursed peacefully, his little blond sprigs of hair twirled around a finger, his placid expression the very calling card of an angel.

Linda was at her best in those nurturing moments. Her

mothering instincts captured the ideal I had envisioned on the beach before we were married, and during our idyllic times with Alana before Kathryn. But the impulse to nurse that I experienced with Alana in my first year of fatherhood had evaporated in the boiling heat of Kathryn's illness. I was now content to watch. Besides, Linda needed and deserved the respite from the unrelenting pressure of medicines and therapies in the forced march of special-needs mothering and being the principal breadwinner. The times for nursing stood like islands in a sea of trouble. It gave me comfort to see the two of them at peace, as if nursing would magically make things better for Eric as it had for Kathryn during that critical period three years earlier when Linda pumped, and I shuttled the special elixir from home to intensive care.

"We were headed back to normal," I whispered one evening as we lay together, arm in arm, the kids asleep. "We have to stay strong."

She sighed, heavily. "I'm tired of staying strong." Each breath pushed out a fresh wave of despair.

Neither of us mentioned the pledge of "no matter what," the night three years earlier that we thought might be Kathryn's last. Instead, we stared into a gloom, tightness gripping our throats and silent tears creeping down our cheeks. We held each other more tightly. The moment of nursing bliss was only one, small velvety car of peace in a long train of despair.

The condition of my kids proved that things weren't normal, and nothing I could do would correct that. I found myself going over the edge one Saturday afternoon at home.

I carried Eric in my left arm. He was wrapped in a cotton

blanket, his blond hair sprouting out like corn silk. I heard a commotion upstairs. As I left the kitchen, the tension was palpable. I ran up, apprehensive about what I was going to encounter. Linda and Kathryn were in a tiff. I entered, aiming to calm things down, feeling that Kathryn needed protecting.

Linda had been patient with Kathryn for hours and was teetering on the edge of exasperation. She shouted at me. "Every time I try to teach them something, you get in the way!"

A steam pipe burst inside me. "Yes, I guess it's time for me to get in the way," I blurted out then stormed out.

The fuss between Linda and Kathryn was minor—not uncommon, but not serious.

What was serious was my feeling of boiling over inside, like my dad, steaming when the car wouldn't start. I was angry, fed up. Too many of these scenes were happening and I felt powerless to balance the equation. Now I had boiled over.

I stumbled into the living room with Eric cradled in one arm. My mind was fogged, my body captured by the cognitive dissonance of struggle and confusion, frustrated with Linda and the kids, frantic about our circumstances and stabbed by the awareness that clashes between Linda and me were the last things the kids needed to witness.

I kicked some empty cardboard boxes. They flew in jumbled disarray. My father showed me this. Inanimate objects get in the way. Move them, shove them, slam them, throw them, kick them out of the way. "God damn it. Fuck it." I thrashed my way through the boxes resting innocently there. My actions reminded me of my father in moments of exasperation. Once, frustrated that he couldn't make it work, he threw a car jack forcefully down to the ground, angry at it. Now Eric was riding an out-of-control dad. I began a motion to throw the obstacles aside. I made a sharp rotation at the hip, as though wading through a swamp, furious at those things blocking me. The motion carried Eric around in centrifugal force, almost throwing him.

Stop! Get ahold of yourself!

I gasped. I caught myself the second before he would have been launched. I went to one knee, suspending my aggression like a gladiator realizing he was fighting himself, my head down, Eric still cradled, safe.

That was too close.

I teared up, contemplating the catastrophe in my life, the near tragedy I had just barely avoided. I don't remember my father coming into my mind at the time, but I see him clearly now. I was overwrought, much like he had been returning from long journeys on the road, unprepared for the internal pressures and anxiety of fathering. I caught a glimpse of what it must have been like for him.

I did what I had to do, took a knee, counted to ten, and breathed deeply.

IN THE VALLEY OF THE MOON

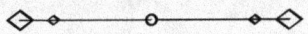

I often read or told bedtime stories at night to the kids. After she turned three, Kathryn joined in the practice of reading, a ritual she and I would enjoy for decades. By the time she was four, Kathryn fell in love with H. A. Rey's *Curious George*. Every night, that little monkey became a partner in preparing for the sandman. Problem was, she never wanted to give up on a story, or rather wanted to hear the story, any George story, again and again. So, I would read it over and over, cherishing, at least in the beginning, the wide eyes and giggles that the George stories engendered in her.

"Will you read it the whole time, Daddy?" she asked. Kathryn used the phrase "the whole time" to mean something between "while you're here with me" and "until I'm fast asleep" or even indefinitely, as in, "don't stop, ever." There was nothing about an expanse of time Kathryn seemed to comprehend, like, say, twenty minutes or an hour for reading or doing any task. Her phraseology displayed a vague grasp of time as a definite quantity. It was charming in some ways and maddening in others, for instance, when trying to set limits on her play time or homework in later years.

I took the time to read slowly, to point to the page, her face close to my hand, as we lay on her bed at night. I drew pleasure and a sense of well-being to see her light up at George's outrageous adventures. She was not just alive; she was reacting like normal kids. In her first year, she sometimes flamed out, walking around with a weightless gaze produced by drugs aimed at controlling her seizures. But with stories, she flickered to life. Her emotional flights with George's adventures gave me a lift. Ironically, given her first months in intensive care, one of her favorite George stories took place in a hospital. The little monkey ate a piece of a board puzzle. An ambulance rushed him to the hospital, where his naughtiness played out. He stole the doctor's stethoscope, delighting children in the story—and Kathryn—as he careened down the hallway in a wheelchair. Kathryn squealed at those scenes each and every time I read them.

"Read it again, Daddy!" She looked up at me, her face shining with a grin as wide as the moon. "Read it again."

After a year, she had memorized a few of those stories and would correct me if I made a slip in reading. Eventually, I taped my reading of the stories, and after reading once or twice out loud, would turn on the tape recorder for her to listen to while Dad could get some sleep, too. By the time she was five, she began taping herself. She wasn't really reading, but she knew enough to turn the pages at the proper time as she recounted the story from memory. Kathryn was a puzzle. She had trouble remembering something from five minutes earlier but could remember long sequences of narrative in stories.

In the summer of 1987, when she was six, I took Kathryn on a special school outing for families whose kids attended Kathryn's Montessori school. We drove north to a camp near Jack London's Valley of the Moon in Sonoma County. The setting might have been in a Disney kid's movie. Redwood groves blanketed low dips in the mountains. Oak, bay, pine, and madrone trees covered the more open hills. We played board and parlor games with other children in the evenings in a lodge by the fire. During the day, we had our choice of activities to do together—horseback riding, croquet, badminton, and swimming. Kathryn was too young and not in command of her muscle coordination enough to take part in team sports on par with other kids. We often watched from the sidelines and talked about what we saw. I explained the broad outlines of games like softball and soccer. Later, we found other parents and kids on a glade and settled in a circle to play cards.

On the first night, we cuddled by an open fire with a group of kids and parents. Someone sang songs and played a guitar. We were wrapped in a magical air without a care in the world. When the fire died down, we stared at the sky sparkling with stars.

"Kathryn, when I was your age, your uncle Kent and I slept in our back yard on warm summer evenings and stared at these stars." Kathryn and I took in the magnificent scene overhead. "We thought, gosh, those stars must be bigger than a house!" I waited for Kathryn's reaction.

She sat silently, and soon her gaze fell onto my face. "Does anyone live there?" she asked.

"No sweetheart. The stars are much bigger than a house, they just sit there, all by themselves… the whole time." I tightened my arm around her shoulder and drew her closer to me.

At last, we went to a little cabin Kathryn and I had all to ourselves under tall pines. The chill of the night crept in, and we crawled into our sleeping bags, cuddling closely on a wide, wooden bunk.

The following morning after breakfast, Kathryn wanted to go to the pool. She had taken to water easily from the very first moments of family outings and had become water safe. But the pool water in the camp was very cold, and the kids mostly sat around the edge dipping, and then withdrawing, their feet in the frigid water. Kathryn bent over to put a finger in. She recoiled and ran back to me with her arms wrapped round her torso. "Brrrr…" she squeaked. "Too cold."

Early the next day, some of her friends from school, who were drawn to Kathryn's sunny disposition, invaded our cabin in a friendly way as we began to stir.

"Good morning, Kathryn. Time to get up," they called, giggling playfully. One of them added, "We want you to be the first one in the pool." They knew that Kathryn was a good swimmer. "Yes, Kathryn, we want to see you swim."

"You guuuyyys," Kathryn demurred, as they drew close, pleading with her.

Kathryn propped herself up on the bed, her hair a tousled mess. She smiled at the attention, taking pride in her skill at swimming.

I shooed the girls out so that Kathryn could get dressed. "We'll meet you at the pool after lunch," I called to them as they paraded out the door.

Early in the afternoon, we reached the pool to find a crowd of kids, some of them already splashing about. Rather than jump in, and without prompting, Kathryn stepped up on the low diving board. Eyes turned to her and everyone fell silent. Kathryn walked calmly out to the end, studying the water, her hands clasped to her chest. The few kids in the pool maneuvered to the edges. No one yet had dived off the board. Kathryn stood there, contemplating the scene. A few calls of prompting grew to a chorus of cheers. Her girlfriends shouted encouragement. She turned to me.

"You can do it, Kathryn," I said quietly, nudging her forward with a head nod.

She edged closer to the edge of the board. She looked around again at the crowd, hearing shouts of support, then to me. Kathryn paused another elastic moment.

She dove.

The children erupted in cheers, many in awe, including her dad. Water from her splash flew about, but the drops on my face were not from the pool. Parents and kids stared in amazement and pleasure, clapping and yelling. Kathryn swam to the ladder. She trotted over to the towel I held, her chest a little further out than usual, shivering and beaming in the attention. She looked up into my eyes.

"Daddy, can we stay at the pool?" she asked. "Will you stay here the whole time?"

* * *

Just before he turned four in 1988, Eric was fitted with

hearing aids. Kathryn had already been wearing them for a year. The introduction of electro-mechanical contraptions made a large dent in the rhythm and discipline of our lives. He and his sister entered a new routine every morning and every evening; caring for hearing aids—those alien, unwanted contraptions—replacing batteries, fitting them into the ear canal, getting used to the intrusive presence of large plastic devices that separated them from their older sister and their playmates. The hearing aids became an emblem of disabilities, a visible badge that we simultaneously detested and needed.

Inside, I hoped they would somehow bring a cure for our problems, but they could not. Yes, they helped. The children were immediately more attentive and alert. There was less yelling; communication improved. Perhaps they helped Eric with auditory processing by clarifying the sounds. But hearing aids magnify every sound, so I am still not so sure the aids my children had were a giant leap forward. Some help, yes, but not a leap. And, in addition to the stigma and the discomfort, there was another downside. For the youngsters, losing hearing aids was very easy.

Returning from an outing one afternoon, making our way to the house from the street, Linda stopped in her tracks, frozen.

"Kathryn. Where are your hearing aids?" Her inquiry was close to interrogation. Kathryn froze.

A wave of guilt broke over her face. "I… I had them a while ago." Her voice trailed off. Her face melted into a puzzlement.

There were two thousand reasons to keep close track.

Insurance covered only one loss per year, and that had already happened. Distractible and with a short-term memory deficit, it was harder for Kathryn to keep track, to register the physical sensation of having them become dislodged, or to remember that she had taken them out.

We all did a collective about-face. Linda was exasperated. For her, a lost set would mean taking on more work to cover the cost of replacements.

"Ice cream for the finder!" I announced, jumping in to redirect the collective mood. We all set about on a safari, retracing our steps to find the hearing aids. All the way across the yard, down the to the street, through plants, bushes, and flowers, right to the curb we trundled, eyes fixed on the ground.

They were in the junipers. It was another last straw for Linda, and with good reason. Linda had opened a professional practice to help cover costs, still earning the lion's share of our household income. For Linda, lost hearing aids felt like going backward, time was lost, new pressure was added. And it was, in a way. Occasionally, something like this would put her over the edge, just as I gone over the edge carrying Eric through the cardboard box jungle in our living room.

After the juniper incident, dental floss became the first line of defense against hearing aid loss. Linda tied dental floss to the left hearing aid, laid the trailing edge around the back of the neck to the right hearing aid, and then attached the bitter end to the collar by safety pin. In our family, a nine-inch length of floss did more good preventing the loss of hearing aids than it ever did for dental hygiene.

* * *

Despite the kids' disabilities, we were determined not to give in to the haunting emptiness, the feeling that something was missing, something was taken from us. The two back-to-back blows staggered us but we were focused on repair, and where no repair was possible, to compensate, and where no compensation was possible, to recall the pledge we had made to ourselves when Kathryn was an infant at the edge of death.

"Remember?" Linda said. "No matter what." I took a deep breath.

"Yes." I looked into her tearing eyes. "To give her everything . . ."

Now we were facing the reality of coping with a family life unalterably different from the one of our dreams. But we didn't dive into a nihilistic emptiness. We fought back. We had good educations and were young and resourceful. Yes, we had many tearful nights. Yes, we fell into dark moods grappling with a sense of loss. But we didn't lose focus. Our resilience took root in the deep connection we had with our children. Linda again and again demonstrated the same strength and resolve she had shown nurturing Kathryn in infancy. She possessed a towering will to muster this power. She continued to nurse Eric on demand. It offered protection and comfort, her way of mending a cosmic injury.

* * *

Each day called for a recalibration in handling the kids: to remind Kathryn of the plan for the day, for the hour; to speak louder and more clearly; for Linda and me to remind ourselves that Alana was now in the minority, and having to put up with special needs that no one could prepare a ten-year-old child to completely understand. She was stellar, and her reaction muted, her accommodation quietly sympathetic. But I worried that deep inside she was struggling with her own questions of how to be a good sister. Nothing in my playbook gave me guidance about how to mentor her, prepare her, educate her about the struggles her siblings were going through, much less about the toll on her parents' marriage.

I saw myself traveling a bumpy arc of fatherhood. I had succeeded for the most part in avoiding the worst aspects of my dad's parenting. But putting into practice the idea of a softer fatherhood was tricky. I hadn't been able to find my feet as a surfer of emotional waves. Instead, on occasion, that naked, blind aggression had come out; I had failed as watchman of the Phantom's mischief. Instead of manifesting my idyllic Dad image, I felt like a soldier on the march with only a vague glimmer of direction, grasping for a few tattered threads of his ideals, trudging through the tedium of medication, hearing aids, tutoring, seemingly endless therapies, and mounting tensions with Linda.

In place of the teddy bear I'd dreamed about stood a grimacing figure holding his arms to the sky trying vainly to ward off any looming trouble. My fatherhood project had arced far from my dream. But it carried me closer to what I felt the kids needed. Meanwhile, we were teetering on the edge of financial ruin. I had pledged to get a real job—something with a steady salary and good health benefits.

PART IV

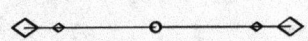

CREATING A NEW LIFE

THE MOVE TO CHEVY CHASE

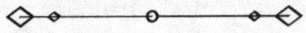

After a bumpy six years of crisis and wobbly routine, we settled into a pattern of caring for both Kathryn and Eric. Days and weeks were filled with steady sessions of therapies in speech (and movement for Kathryn), regular tending to hearing aids, plus special needs consultations with physicians in Berkeley and Oakland. Yes, there were picnics, outings, and play dates. Visits to Mom and Kent in Sacramento helped soften our transition into the new reality of disabilities. But, nagging reminders of the not-normal dogged us.

Wherever we went, there always seemed to be a need for explanations, the making of exceptions, and fiddling with excuses when the kids didn't respond as playmates might have expected or when adults went unanswered by one kid or the other. We simply got used to the idea that a few warnings were necessary. I often felt like I was overdoing it, being a broken record in offering information to neighbors, newcomers, and even strangers. My kids had special needs, I had to explain. It became matter of fact, but it never felt natural.

Partly in reaction, my identity shifted subtly. A nesting

instinct came out. We worked assiduously on every aspect of our wonderful house in Berkeley. We were lucky to acquire it—a beauty from the 1920s with fine architectural detail. We had won it at auction at an estate sale. *The last move we'll ever need to make,* I had thought.

We dived into fix-up mode, half aware that our house was the only thing in our lives that we *could* fix. I deployed my modest construction skills to convert the basement to a studio for an au pair. We splashed color here and there. Alana's room got bright Marimekko curtains. I wrapped a big bulletin board in fire-engine red burlap for Kathryn's room. We found a woven basket swing, like an elongated half-eggshell. I suspended it from our bedroom ceiling to have a swinging cradle at the foot our bed. With each child, a whimper or cry was just a soft foot-stroke away from a gentle swing, calming everybody in the room. I hung a cotton hammock in our bedroom and snapped a picture of the three little ones peering out like baby chicks in a nest. It still hangs in my office as a reminder now, as it was at the time, of a dream of normalcy in our jumbled-up lives.

We were nearing our last year of health insurance coverage at Linda's workplace. We took a second mortgage on the house and set about constructing a deck with a room underneath for a rental. The activity itself was a tonic. One afternoon, the five of us gathered at the windows and watched a monstrous drill rig on half-tracks maneuver up the path to within feet of our viewing spot. Little Eric and big Dad were enthralled with the giant yellow machine churning away, so far from the streets, so close to the house. It began boring

deep columns in the front yard for foundations. The Irani-
an structural engineer I had hired showed confidence in his
calculations. Before pouring the cement col-umns, I asked the
city inspector for his impression of the thirteen shafts that
were now sprouting rebar in our front yard.

"They go down sixteen feet to bedrock," he said dryly.

"Will it hold for earthquakes?" I asked the inspector.

He looked at me with a small smile. "This deck will hold
up the whole hillside."

We weren't just nesting, we were building a bomb shelter
against the next virus. We were putting extra-soft feathering
to compensate for the sharp edges that protruded into our
lives—the medication regime, misunderstandings, the emotional demands, the tensions and fights. Despite and perhaps
because of that, our house was becoming a home instead of a
hospital. We were determined to improve the house and protect ourselves. The busy-ness brought us satisfaction: something new was replacing something broken.

* * *

A year of searching for my "real job" with countless
applications finally paid off, sort of. At last, our pathway into
continued insurance coverage was within reach. Three job offers arrived. The problem was they were all on the East Coast.
This presented a glum choice: a trade-off of relief for Linda
from working to cover medical indebtedness, in exchange for
leaving our new nest and moving across country. After much
discussion, I accepted the World Bank offer.

Linda and I had begun to shape a vision. It was 1988.

Perhaps we could move for three to five years, build up a business practice, and then return to California and resume consulting from Berkeley. One of my colleagues at UC Berkeley said, "No, man. Ride it out. Do your time and take your pension." I couldn't imagine that. "No way," I replied. "That's way too long a stretch." The Berkeley home, the sheltered nest into which we had invested so much, where all the kids were born, the battleground where we had fought to save Kathryn, for better or for worse, that was to be the place for us in the long haul. Much was still at stake. I couldn't be sure of the long-term outcome for Kathryn. We still had a long road to travel. But Berkeley remained my homing point, a base to which I had to return sooner or later.

* * *

The day arrived in May for my departure to Washington. Linda and the kids would have to join me later, after the children completed the academic term. I was facing nine months alone in DC. I called the taxi. The air was heavy, like a funeral. I pulled my things together in the living room. Everyone was morose, the kids and Linda in tears. I readied myself by the door for the cab. When I bent over to pick up my bags, I put my face into a vase of reeds, one of which went into my eye. It stung, as though I inadvertently inflicted pain to recruit comfort and solace.

In Washington, I leased a small apartment as a transitional residence while I started work at the World Bank. I ameliorated the longing in the separation by judicious selection of work assignments that would allow me to piggy-back travel to

California every month or so. That, with telephone calls, somehow got us through, but not smoothly. The kids were troubled, even though they understood. They knew an adventure would come the fol-lowing year when the whole family would join Dad in Washington. Alana was steady, Kathryn inquisitive, and Eric nonplussed.

I eagerly spoke on the phone with the kids.

"Daddy," Alana said with excitement and anticipation, "do I get my own room in Washington? I want palm trees and flamingos—you know, the inflatable ones."

"Hi, Dad," Kathryn would say. "When will we see you?" Kathryn couldn't comprehend the physical distance between us. She continued to show confusion about the concept of time. She would often say, "Will you be with us the whole time?" I think she meant "Will this separation ever end?"

With Eric, I struggled to keep a connection going. As natural for a four-year-old, he responded to my questions, but rarely initiated them. Invariably, he would end the conversation like this: "OK, I'm done now." Silence. I felt a small collapse inside. The separation was adding an extra challenge to my fathering him. My father had never called from his road trips. At least I was trying. But it wasn't working very well. My fatherhood project was taking another hit. What else could I do? I called more, sent cards and presents, and made the most of the few times we could manage to reunite on business travel, vacations, and holidays.

* * *

The following summer, 1989, Linda piled the kids and an

au *pair* into our van and began the journey east. I knew that she had started out north on a coastal route, but after several days of hearing nothing, I grew concerned. I called her friends. I called some family on the West Coast. No one had been in touch. Then I called the highway patrol in California.

"No sir, we have no reported accidents matching the description of your car," the operator said. The same message came in from Washington and Oregon. Finally, I rang up the Royal Canadian Mounted Police.

"Yes, ma'am. A 1985 white Aerostar van with a lady driver and four passengers," I reported, trying to be calm.

"Excuse me, sir. You're an American, right?"

"Yes, ma'am."

"Do you realize how many calls we get about missing vehicles every day? Every day," she said.

"Yes, ma'am, I know you're a big country."

"That's right, for your information, we're bigger than the continental United States."

"Yes, ma'am."

The following morning my phone rang.

"You'll never believe this," Linda said, laughing.

"Where the hell have you been? I've been worried sick!" I blurted, without letting her answer. "Why are you laughing?" I paused. "Let me guess, red jackets on horseback. Royal Canadian Mounted Police. They found you, right?"

"No," she said, finishing a laughing breath. "A giant twenty-four-wheeler pulled up next to us on the highway at sixty miles an hour." She was chuckling. "I heard a couple of really loud blasts from his horn," she said. "Then his partner leaned out the window, held up a CB radio, then cupped his hands around his mouth and yelled: 'Are you Linda Campbell?'" I nodded my head in the affirmative; then the guy said, 'Call your husband.'"

Linda had made leisurely stops in Seattle, Vancouver, Banff, and other places, driving early in the morning while the kids slept and spending long afternoons taking in the sights. She hadn't called because she was on a mission—taking her time, engineering fun for the kids, not worrying about me.

* * *

Shortly after moving to Washington, I found a small condo as our temporary residence for when Linda and the kids arrived and until we could find a more permanent place for the family. The kids were eleven, eight, and four. Our place was a glorified one bedroom, all of us sleeping in one room.

Every morning, Alana would get herself up, put on the uniform of the private school she was attending, and make her way to the bus stop. It was just another routine Alana managed on her own, never complaining. She did everything that needed to be done.

Linda and I attended to the details of Kathryn and Eric. For a long time, I felt bad, thinking Alana was left so much to her own devices. She insists now that she liked the independence and sense of freedom and responsibility. She says it made her readier for her teen years.

But as a father, I felt like a failure. My instincts were to be there more, to fulfill my pledge to be available and nurturing.

* * *

In the middle of the night late in August, Linda found Kathryn motionless, sweating profusely under her blankets.

"I felt her thrashing," Linda said in a kind of defeated way. "I pulled back her blankets. She was soaked."

I was still a little hazy, coming out of sleep. Linda riveted on me.

"I think she's had a *grand mal* seizure."

"I'll call an ambulance," I said. The adrenalin came on suddenly. I fumbled trying to hit 9-1-1 smoothly. Suppressing my anxiety was even harder.

"We need an ambulance at the Willoughby... Seizure... Eight-year-old," I blurted out.

The operator spoke in a cool and mechanical tone, comforting in an odd sort of way. My throat was dry, my mind racing. *What more can I do? Is her life dangling again at the end of a string?* I glanced at Linda holding Kathryn in a limp pile across her lap. Eric and Alana were still asleep. The short wait seemed like hours. The EMTs knocked. "I'll go with her," I said. Linda nodded.

I crawled into the darkened ambulance and sat on the bench in the small compartment next to my daughter. Oxygen bottles, drip lines, packages of medications and dressings hung from the ambulance walls. My watch read three a.m. We pulled onto the darkened streets.

"Don't go to sleep on me, Kathryn," the EMT kept saying as we sped through the night toward the hospital. Her eyes were closing and opening slowly. The compartment lights shone dimly, casting a red hue. I could see her matted hair, still damp from perspiration, her face pallid and sagging. I sat next to her, numb, utterly exposed, riding blindly into the night. The lurching ambulance was like our life with Kathryn, careening through darkness, unable to see the path ahead, not knowing how much further we were to travel.

My mind ran back to the night my father died. I was at newborn Kathryn's bedside, holding her quivering little fingers through a seizure, while a hundred miles away, my father's heart was shuddering to a stop. Now, eight years later, we were hurtling again to an unknown destination. The thought of my father dying after Kathryn's survival inured me to the next unforeseen catastrophe lurking down the road. Perhaps it would strike in the hospital during the next tachycardia. I numbly searched for an emotional wall to hide behind for the next hit.

In the lurching ambulance, my insides were wrung into a small, tight knot. I fought the snuffing out of the last flickering dreams of a normal family. I gave way to the EMTs as they adjusted the drip and monitored Kathryn's blood pressure. I held my head in my hands as we jostled through the streets. My emotional life rode on Kathryn's drip line. I felt the tension in my jaw, as if bracing for another neurological storm. How many more storms will there be? My fathering was just a matter of being there, reacting to every new twist and turn.

Kathryn had had many seizures in the first few years of life. They came under control with medication, but with each dose, we were making a nasty bargain. The seizures gradually disappeared, but the medications ate away at her vitality. We were caught in an emotional vice, squeezed by the fear of seizures on one side, and on the other, the fears about the long-term impact of medications. I can't tell from my perspective now whether I was making a mistake at the time about medications. For the most part, we were drawn to go with the expert advice. Yet I felt that we had made the right calls by gradually weaning Kathryn from phenobarb and, when she was still an infant, denying permission for that biopsy. Those decisions were made on gut instinct. But now that the seizures had returned, I was no longer sure about my intuition.

The ambulance pulled into the emergency room entrance. We were shuttled into the hospital. Kathryn caught sight of me walking beside her gurney. I held her hand. The look on her face was a blend of panic, confusion, and delirium. It was the same for me. Then a small shine crept into her eye. She squeezed my hand. The knot in my stomach released. I knew we were out of the woods.

Kathryn was discharged the following morning. I reached work by midday. Linda managed to shield the kids from our distress. Getting back to our routine was like climbing onto a jostling roller coaster. There was nothing smooth about it; every day was a lurching ride through life, another surprise just over the next rise.

* * *

Six months after the family joined me in Washington, we caught the first glimpse of our new house in Chevy Chase— even before we knew it was going to be ours. We attended a party on the snowy night of New Year's Eve 1989. A beautiful street was lined with hundred-foot beeches and oaks. Holiday lights twinkled off the snow. Linda and I fell in love with the area right away. That night was a magical introduction to our new neighborhood. Some months later, a house on that block came up for sale as an estate auction. Linda suggested that we write letters about our family to the person selling the house. He accepted our offer over many others. The estate sale was ratified in court.

But before we could move in, even before the kids could see our new house, we had to do lots of patching and repair— lath and plaster had fallen from the entry hall ceiling, the house was overgrown on two sides; it looked to be succumbing to ghosts. But in short order we had it in shape and settled into what we all regarded as a temporary residence, for four or five years, before we would be able to move back to California.

The search for the new house and the subsequent fixing up proved to be another therapy we didn't appreciate at the time. Repairing, remodeling, expanding, buying second hand furniture, and adding color all proved to be hidden forms of healing. A little like rivets under the bridge, they helped us put things back together.

We made new rooms for the kids, giving them a new perspective. I built a bunk bed for Kathryn and Eric. We expanded and refinished the attic and turned it into the largest room in the house for Alana. At last, she received something special: the largest, the highest up, all her own. Our re-nesting lasted a couple of years.

Meanwhile, Linda took the lead in finding schools for the kids. She was good at it, searching out the right combination of attributes to fit each child's circumstances. It was like college visits, only more intense and time-consuming. She tirelessly turned over every rock. For Alana and Eric, she found good fits in private schools where they were likely to get more individual attention, small class size, and enrichment opportunities.

Alana easily gained admission at a suburban school for girls on a beautiful campus. Faculty and administration members made it clear that while academics in private schools were important, character development was also given high priority. And although the student body included a princess from Thailand and many daughters of millionaires, the focus on character and individual attention outweighed the absence of economic, racial, and ethnic diversity that she might've found in public schools.

For Eric, the first hurdle was to find a primary school that would feed into any one of several private schools for grades four and above. Prospective pupils came from very well-to-do and politically and socially well-connected families, so demand for the school we wanted was high. Though the administration had some qualms about Eric's hearing needs, he was admitted with help from his high IQ scores and sunny personality. The kindergarten teacher loved Eric, and the school responded to his special needs with auditory equipment worn by both the teacher and Eric which broadcast her voice directly to Eric's hearing aids.

The clunky receiver hanging around Eric's neck exacerbated the stigma of his hearing aids. One day, an open mic helped soothe that hurt. The teacher was abruptly called out of class to be informed that the school pet had died. She inadvertently left her mic on as she was informed about the loss, allowing Eric to hear the conversation among teachers. That episode made Eric the only kid in the know as he relayed the news to his classmates.

After the first year, the administration expressed concern about its ability to offer accommodations, and we worried about whether he would be invited back. Linda took the lead on persuading the administrators, convincing them to take the risk.

By grade three, the natural next school for Eric was a brother institution to Alana's girls' school. Neither of the schools had other disabled kids, but Linda thought she would have more sway and be able to mobilize help for Eric better there than in public school. That proved to be correct. Once Eric made it through the demanding feeder school, he was admitted to that next-level private school.

For Kathryn, no private school in California or Washington was able to meet her particular needs. After exploring special needs schools in the greater DC area, Linda found that the public schools in Montgomery County, Maryland, were a good fit for her. That was another reason that our house on the magical street—nestled in Montgomery County—was so right.

Public education in Maryland provided for a wide range of students. Linda had ferreted this out, and she quickly mastered the system for obtaining support for kids with disabilities. She was diligent and tireless in following up every lead. Each semester in Kathryn's school, a resource team would draw up an individual educational plan for Kathryn, a specific, written strategy tailored for her.

Early in the process, a principal had suggested that a full graduation might not be in the cards for Kathryn. Linda would have none of this.

No prejudging, Linda insisted. "She has to fail first." The educators fell silent. Linda attended every meeting and was an advocate for Kathryn, ensuring that she be given every single resource to which she was entitled. The law made provisions for children like Kathryn, but parents had to fight, sometimes with legal help, to ensure that the full benefits of the system were made available. Linda won every step of the way.

* * *

Along with the educational plans came the scheduling of speech and occupational therapy for both Kathryn and Eric.

"Watch my lips, Kathryn, and try to repeat what I say," the speech therapist said. She would come to the house three times a week and run through a series of oral exercises with Kathryn. Her hearing impairment had produced speech deficits much like Eric's.

"The cat ran after the rat," the therapist enunciated.

"The cath ran after the rath," Kathryn parroted.

I sat behind Kathryn as the therapist looked closely into Kathryn's face and exaggerated her lips. Kathryn's consonant stops were slurred, but she was getting better by the month. Kathryn wasn't sure what she was supposed to do but was earnest and compliant. She would do whatever she was asked, even without knowing why. Her progress provided relief. In this one area, we were heartened to see improvement.

Eric had a different challenge. The therapist would sit in front of him and conceal her mouth with a small piece of paper. The idea was to induce Eric to listen intently to what she was saying, rather than reading her lips. It seemed like a torturous form of therapy for Eric. I would sometimes see beads of sweat on his forehead, his brow furrowed, as he listened. It was gut-wrenching to see him struggle, but all I could do was heap praise on Eric after each session and encourage him to keep going, that his hearing and understanding were improving. In retrospect, I cannot be sure the therapy helped.

MORNING IN CHEVY CHASE

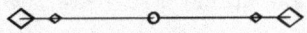

In 1990, on a typical Campbell family day in Chevy Chase, Belle, our fluffy white Bichon Frise, bounded into Eric's room for a good morning face-licking. (Eric later wrote a short paper in his third-grade class about his small, white alarm clock on four legs.) Belle's morning appearance triggered the soft whir of household chaos spinning into motion. Eric, now five, was the first up. He strayed into our bathroom and hit three out of four walls peeing before he realized it was too late to be tidy. Then he pushed into bed next to Linda, while I pulled on Levis, a shirt, and shoes. Nothing else. It was not worth trying to get more clothes on for the a.m. routine. For this first stage of morning, I had to fly lean.

I kissed Eric gently on the head and drifted into Kathryn's room to give her a tender cuddle and get her stirring.

"Good morning, sweetheart," I said in a low voice. She rolled over, her back to me. "I'll be back in a jiffy with the magic potion." She knew what was happening but didn't reply.

The real truth in my maneuver was to get my potion—the caffeine bean—as well as hers. My small, personalized routine helped order the day. It was as if this rhythm, this predictabil-

151

ity,made up for so many uncontrollable forces in our lives, like seizures, school performance pressures, broken hearing aids, insults from schoolmates. It was my way, my order in a teacup, to keep me grounded.

The coffee itself was almost always a disappointment; it was the routine that counted. I stirred a few tablespoons of whole milk, some turbinado, and a dollop of molasses into my art deco "Miami—A State of Mind" cup. I poured the first tranche of coffee through the grounds an extra time, to get that additional bite of flavor and jolt of the bean.

As I prepared a small tray to carry Ovaltine (Kathryn's magic potion), I dreamed about my days in Berkeley, stirring my Peet's coffee till ten, feeling the small warmth of sun coming over the Berkeley hills thawing the morning chill, as I savored the distant eucalyptus aroma, and gazed at the *Chronicle* with the deep satisfaction of knowing that nothing of great journalistic value would escape me. The tone of those California mornings was set by the pleasant prospect of noodling a consultant report or dictating into a tape recorder by the local pool till it was time to trade lap pool for carpool, or to take over with the kids after nap time.

Kathryn's tray also held her morning medicines. She was then beginning to take Depakote, prescribed after her seizure the previous fall. At the time, Depakote was a new drug that didn't have the downsides of phenobarb but did have its own dangerous side effects on the liver, especially for infants and toddlers. There we were, in the dark again, struggling to weigh the costs and benefits of a medication without complete information. Physicians will tell you that seizures do not have long-term effects. But watching your young child go through the shaking, the eyes rolled up, the unconscious thrashing, will make you want to reach for any palliative. We saw Depakote as a short- to medium-term therapy, even though we were still uncertain as to how to think about the seizures themselves.

Depakote came in a capsule. We had learned long ago the futility of getting a capsule of anything down Kathryn (for instance, medications for ear infection). Instead, I assembled my drug administration tools—the tray, the capsule, a spoon, a couple of tablespoons of lemon yogurt, the Ovaltine, a paper towel and my second cup of coffee—and headed up the stairs.

"Kathryn, I've got your Ovaltine," I announced as I entered the room. She was in the exact same position as when I left her. "Scoot over, sweetie." I settled beside her and brought her up to sitting position. She had the rag doll look, hair mussed, muscles limp, playing possum. I put the cup to her lips.

"Here, smell this. . . . Take a sip." Her nose twitched. She couldn't resist. Once she got a few ounces in her, she began to stir. I spooned out a small portion of yogurt, opened the capsule of Depakote and carefully poured the little white beads onto the bed of yogurt, then slipped the spoon once again sideways into the yogurt container. Small waves of yogurt piled up around the perimeter of the spoon to keep the beads from rolling off.

She turned her head away.

"No, no, come on, sweetie," I said. She frowned. Kathryn practiced one of the few forms of control and manipulation left to her by taking her own sweet time to open up for the medicine. It was easy to understand her stalling, but also easy

153

to get crabby and gruff with her after holding a delivery pose for long minutes. Kathryn wanted and needed to control her world. The more she learned about the world, the more she needed to hold it still, to keep it from spinning out of control, racing beyond her. Stalling and taking time—getting out of bed, getting dressed, exiting the car after a ride, even opening presents—were moments during which Kathryn could slow the world down to her speed, make it bend a bit to her own pace.

Finally, she opened up, and plop, the beads were in. It was not always that easy. Many days she would stammer and push it away, the yogurt and beads falling into a mess on her PJs or sheets. That made me upset on so many levels. First, we needed to merge Kathryn's pace with our own. Most of the time I felt irritated that we were falling out of step with the day, with the time we had for breakfast, with the schedule for the oncoming school bus, or, at other times, with the friends and classmates who might be waiting for the party to start—Kathryn's party. And angry, because every day, every night, without fail, we had to administer this entropic contradiction that itself was liable to do long-term damage. And yet there was no other way to manage the multiple conditions affecting Kathryn. Yogurt beads. Little plastic pill organizers. Dental floss hearing aid tethers, Post-its: all small tools we used against the disorder of our life.

* * *

I could hear Linda darting around in the other room, getting Eric dressed. He was quiet as she pulled on his shirt and gathered his shoes and mismatched socks. He left the room to get a matched pair. A minute later, I heard Eric running to his mother, sobbing, panic and fear in his voice.

"What is it, honey?" He burrowed into her embrace, his sobs and anguish bubbling out. At last, comforted, his composure returned, but his voice was still choked with shock.

"It's ha- ha- ha-ppening," he stammered, his eyes flooded with tears.

"What's happening, sweetie?"

"My hearing is going." He searched her face as if appealing to the gods. Linda looked down at him, the wisdom of motherhood in full force. She knew his fears were real, but not his diagnosis.

"Let me have your hearing aids," she said softly. Eric pulled them from their perch and handed them to her. "Where were you when you noticed this?" she asked him, comfortingly.

"In my room, getting socks." A warm smile spread over Linda's face.

"Angel," she cooed, "your hearing isn't going." He locked onto her eyes as if hearing a suspended sentence. "Honey, your batteries are petering out."

Eric's fears were raw and near the surface during his early years. We learned from his therapist that he had a fear of death connected to his hearing loss. He concluded in some primitive way that since his sister had nearly died, and also had a hearing loss, that he too faced the prospect of death.

Many times, in my attempts to navigate the arc of fatherhood, I tried silently to probe into Eric's and Kathryn's psyches, wondering what was going through their minds, what kind of world they saw, what threats and fears were hiding there. How different was their world from mine? It never occurred to me that a fear of death lurked in Eric, nor that his sweating one day left him with the paralytic sensation that he was melting. Kathryn must have been constantly confused with a flurry of life racing at her at home, around the dinner table, with her siblings, at school.

The frightening aspects of a world distorted by hearing, intellect, or auditory processing make you want to draw the kids to you and hold them tight, sheltering, consoling, and comforting them, just as Linda had done when Eric's hearing aid batteries died. I discovered later, that too much of that comforting reaction is also a kind of sky-holding that could, in the long run, impede Eric's and Kathryn's ability to manage those confusing and scary moments on their own.

Meanwhile, Alana went about her morning business, quietly getting herself ready for school up in her top-floor room. She darted in and out like a busy executive while the rest of us fussed with matching socks, Depakote, and hearing aid batteries. Alana acted as though she knew that her role had to be an independent one. She liked it in some ways, doing her own readiness thing, calling her friends in the carpool to coordinate the pick-up time, fixing her own breakfast. If I'd had my way, I would have been driving Alana to school. In fact, I did whenever I could. And yet, Alana told me years later that, just like when living at the condo apartment, her independence and responsibility helped build her confidence and strengthened her sense of self-reliance.

"I just adapted, Dad," she said, years later. Then, after a pause, she added, "It made me stronger, and I don't think there was any downside." Ironically, that conclusion went smack up against my fatherly ambition to lean into her emotional life—not to be intrusive, but to be available—to offset some of the discord engendered by her siblings, to be available, to encourage and guide.

Back in my morning routine, I worked with Kathryn, coaxing her through dressing for school.

"Come on Kathryn, time to head downstairs." Her motor, now kick-started by the Ovaltine, was running at a normal pace by now. I paired off with Kathryn, and Linda with Eric, because I would drive Eric to school and have time with him later. Kathryn and I took the stair steps, one by one, hand in hand. Her words came in small, grumpy packages.

"What's for breaky?" she asked.

"Wakkles, frozen wakkles," I replied. "Wakkles" was Kathryn's word for waffles.

"The green ones?" she asked, referring to the green logo on the low-fat box of whole grain waffles.

"That or Mr. Mush," I replied. When the weather was cold, she liked oatmeal, the kind with the Quaker on the container.

"Wakkles," she affirmed.

"Wakkles it is." We reached the kitchen. Linda and Eric would work their way down soon. We were almost never in unison. My ideas about the happy family, in the style of Ozzie and Harriet sitting around the dining room table at mealtimes, were a dim memory. We had little idea about how much support Kathryn would need in life, and even less about how grave Eric's more hidden loss really was—particularly with attendant auditory processing and, as we would learn later, attention deficit hyperactivity disorder.

Small quotidian rhythms like platoon meals, and the larger picture of organic, unified family life, got all jumbled up. In ones and twos, we would eat, sometimes while standing. Instead of five of us around the breakfast table, it was the hearing aids, floss, batteries, lunch boxes, and other school items spread out on the table before the food arrived. Dental floss was tied to the hearing aids and anchored to a safety pin. Batteries and floss ties were checked.

Linda and Eric made their way into the kitchen as Kathryn dug into her waffles.

"Hi, Da-da," Eric chirped in a playful way. "Can I have waffles too?"

"Yes, big boy, but not too much syrup for you. Too much sugar."

"How about honey?"

"OK, but only a little." I spooned out a half tablespoon of honey.

Alana glided in, lending a hand with lunch for her sibs, made her own, and chatted lightly with Kathryn and Eric.

"Good morning, Mr. E," Alana said.

"Hi, Alani."

"Where's your left hearing aid, Eric?" she asked.

"I dunno," he said. "It wasn't on my nightstand." Then he remembered, he was supposed to know. He looked at each of us, frozen in a stare.

"Check your pockets," I said. He rummaged around and pulled it out sheepishly.

"OK, let's tie you up." I draped the dental floss around the back of his neck and pinned it under his collar.

Usually, I would drive Eric to kindergarten, and the last stage in the morning routine was upon me. Time for the check list:

Double-check the floss and pins.

Verify that spare batteries had been put in their assigned places.

Spread the peanut butter.

Tuck the sandwiches into the plastic bags.

Pack the lunches. (Hide a surprise note.)

Write the names on the bags.

Toast the frozen waffles.

Pour the milk.

Glance through the window at the next-door neighbor walking around in her nightie.

Set the table.

Give my coffee another whirl in the microwave.

Glance at the New York Times one last time.

Start the car.

Yell at the kids to put in the hearing aids.

Check again to see if they were finishing the last few bites.

Listen for the diesel rumble of Kathryn's bus.

Run a brush through her hair a second time.

Pass my hand over the top of Eric's head.

Listen again for the bus.

"Kathryn, the bus is here, let's go!"

Once more, Kathryn takes her sweet time getting out the door. Three cars were backed up behind the waiting bus, drivers steaming.

One of the benefits of her special needs program was at-door pickup. As often as not, we had to hurry to meet its arrival. Occasionally, when he was in a bad mood, the bus driver would roar off in a cloud of diesel, leaving us stranded. My anger would flare up. I would reprimand Kathryn. "See, that's why you have to move along. Now how are we going to get you to school?"

"Well . . . won't they . . . come back?"

"No, Kathryn, he's gone. He has to pick up other kids." Kathryn would look down, a shadow of chagrin on her face. She eventually got better at making the bus.

This morning, I gave her a big kiss and hug and answered her fourth round of questions about the plan for the day as I walked her onto the bus. Then back to the house, to get Eric's speech therapy sheets, put them on the dashboard for practice on Wisconsin Avenue, buckle him in, clean the peanut butter off the car door, push my coffee cup into the corner of the floorboard so it wouldn't spill, set the rear-view mirror and my glasses, and put the Volvo in first gear. I took a deep breath. The last phase of the morning routine was coming to an end.

The drive down Wisconsin Avenue was another routine and almost a full day's worth of energy all by itself. This was part of the day I loved to hate, when I most missed California. Drivers in Maryland, Virginia, and Washington reduced a safe change of lanes to a sneering swerve, rather than yield to us innocents politely waiting for an opening with a blinking signal.

Virginia had extended the reckless, me-first age of the nineties into the daily commute. Awful driving was compounded by an international mix of customs at the wheel. An international mix at a bank, a banquet, or a band can be healthy. An international mix in the commute edges into chaos. The duppies (downwardly mobile urban professional) and all the many drivers steeped in Grand Prix racing pull their fantasies into action as they race up and down Connecticut Avenue.

"You idiot!" I declared as a car swerved into my lane. Eric looked across every four or five minutes in response to my muttering and cursing. So much for my hopes of showing Eric lessons in courtesies of fine motoring.

"Idiot," Eric parroted, a grin on his face.

I began the practice sheets for Eric's speech, which still produced slurring. I had often heard him repeat words from speech or hearing specialists in the sound booth, and my heart would sink when I realized how much he missed: "candy," became "kitchen," "hot dog" was "hop along;" and "picnic" "pick up."

I started: "The lion gazed through the grass."(underlining for enunciation.) He repeated pretty well. "The snake hisses at the zebra." On and on we go, sentence after sentence. He almost never complained about this. He seemed to recognize the therapeutic need, much like Alana used to do as we drove to Sausalito for psychoanalytic help after Kathryn's first hospitalization.

As we moved with the DC traffic, I watched the long strings of cheap speed (small, fast, inexpensive cars) bob and weave in front of me, and I took mental note to share with Eric—sometime in the distant future, after the Ninja Turtles had lost their appeal—that the Nobel Prize in chemistry in 1972 went to a Belgian guy who, by observing entropy of ther-mo-chemical reactions, and by probabilistic inference, predict-ed patterns of traffic flow and traffic jams. Traffic management techniques like putting the bank of synchronized traffic lights to dose traffic after the toll booth on the Bay Bridge could be attributed to the Belgian's productive dreaming.

But no such traffic staggering was happening during the morning commute in DC. I wondered then whether any kind of probabilistic inference might help me get through the chaotic mess not just of traffic, but the almost daily stumbling through our routine—lost this or that, spilled yogurt, missed bus, misplaced homework, the constant sprinting just to stay in position.

I would grit my teeth, hoping Eric garnered more from the *hisses* and *grasses* than he did from my grumbling at idiot drivers.

We pulled into the school drop-off zone.

"Give me a hug, big boy." We lingered a moment at the door. I looked into his eyes. A glimmer of apprehension often marked the start of his school day. I felt a small twist in my gut; racing hectically just to get through the morning, then plunging into the mess of traffic, tumbling out at the other end, I realized there in the parking lot that something terribly important had been lost. The really important feelings of the early part of the day had been pushed aside in the hubbub.

"Mom will pick you up this afternoon, E." I called him E when we were together one-on-one. I paused. "Tonight, we'll work on the racer car." He brightened and ran in with his friends.

As a joint project mostly for Eric, I had started to build a life-size wooden race car in the basement.

I headed downtown through another gaggle of undisciplined commuters to join the world of ties and coats for the next nine hours. I grimaced at the memory—before the era of my children back in the seventies—of standing on a corner in downtown San Francisco in my tennis shorts and sports coat silently mocking the suits and ties ebbing and flowing on the streets among office towers. In those days, my pal Rowbear and I played with the idea of buying the caboose down by the produce market in Oakland. We made plans to canoe across the bay to picnic under the Bay Bridge near Treasure Island. Today, instead of caboose and kayak, I put on my tie and made ready for stage two of my day: the working world.

GOD, THE UNIVERSE,
AND VIDEO GAMES

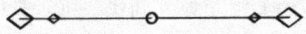

The following summer, Kathryn, Eric, and I motored along in silence for a few minutes, each of us savoring our ice cream on a warm summer day. Eric, just over five years old, and Kathryn, age eight, sat in the back seat admiring their cones, taking slow tastes. We were on a daddy outing following a long "mission" for the World Bank to Latin America. I had instituted an alternative to bringing home gifts after each long trip. The new regime consisted of ice cream and a toy or gift the kids would pick out. We rode with windows down, a warm breeze flowing around us, a feeling of contentment everywhere.

Eric broke the silence, reaching far into the universe.

"Dad, have you ever got you pini caught in your zipper?"

I smiled inwardly and did a mental roll of the eyes.

"Yes, it really hurts, doesn't it?" I said, seriously.

"Yeah. Could you die?"

"No, no, you wouldn't die, but it sure can sting."

"Yeah. I hate it when it stings."

"Me too. That's why I wear these 501s, Eric."

"Huh?"

"My pants. Button fly."

"Can I get button fly?"

"Maybe. I don't know if they make button fly for five-year-olds. Let's check next time we go to the store."

At that point on the arc of fatherhood, I aimed for normal, just a big, fat normal—to be a middle-class dad with middle-class kids. Nothing anomalous to see here. Instead, both Eric and Kathryn continued with speech or occupational therapy two or three times a week. Medical checkups dotted our monthly calendar. The house was home and clinic, and, with Linda's efforts in homework, we ran a special education classroom to boot.

After another few minutes of quiet, ice creams half gone, Kathryn piped up. "Dad. What is church?"

I was not prepared for this one. OK, church, I can handle that, but what about the follow-ups? What about God? The entirety of decades of my own questioning came down to a single question from Kathryn. And I didn't have an answer. I realized right away that the long path I had traveled was a solitary one. All my years of thinking about church-going, religious and philosophical explorations, about religion and God—all those had been kept to myself. Or rather, they had been crowded out by so many other mundane demands of the day. I had left absolutely no waypoints to mark my own journey into ideas of God and religion. Now there was no escaping it. I drew a breath and dived in.

"Some people go because they think God is responsible for everything in the world, so they go to church to worship

God." I glanced at her in the back seat through the rearview mirror to see if she was following me. Her face was scrunched up a bit. "I think of church as a place where you go to be with your family and friends," I followed up. Still silence. Both of them seemed to be taking it in.

I guess I wasn't surprised that my answers weren't hitting home with Kathryn. There was no home. She had no basis for understanding these concepts. One irony in our family was that the kid hit hardest in life—heart condition, epilepsy, kidney shrinkage, hearing loss, brain damage—was the one with the least guile and is most likely to take on all things headfirst. She knew enough to ask but didn't have a basis for comprehending abstract answers.

My lack of preparedness on the religious issue stretched far back. By the time my brother and I were in primary school, Dad occasionally encouraged us to attend Mormon services. He attended services irregularly. Though unequivocal about the appeal of Mormon family and community life, he was ambivalent about the religiosity of Mormonism. Meanwhile, Mom had drifted into part-time Presbyterianism. Sunday school at the Presbyterian church was much more to my liking. But the contrast between the two worlds—the grandiose structure of Mormonism on the one hand, and on the other, the simplicity and light touch of the Presbyterians—struck a chord of curiosity. How could these two protestant religions be so different from each other, not to mention the two of them so different from other religions?

Early in high school, I came across Huston Smith's *Great Religions of the World*. Smith laid it out so plainly. Many peoples around the world have found distinct pathways to god-liness and worship. They had much in common, but the variety persuaded me that choosing one, if any, should be a matter of careful deliberation, not a process of familial osmosis. Godliness came within the framework of being human, not the other way around. But as a father, our internal family discussions hadn't reached very far into the matter. Rather than herding the kids into one or another of the camps in that world as I had been, without any choice in the matter, I decided I would wait for it to come up and let the kids see all the options. Now it was up.

I continued. "I think each and every one of us is respon-sible for ourselves, and so we go to church to celebrate our loving others. You know, like when you feel really warm with love for Mom and Dad?"

"You mean like at Christmas?" Kathryn asked.

"Yeah, OK, like at Christmas." I glanced again in the mirror. She was pensive. "Well, that's God inside of you and you can go to church to be with the people you love, like your family, friends, and neighbors when you feel like that, or when you are sad, and you want to feel like that."

There was a long pause. A few more licks of ice cream. More silence, then Eric again:

"Dad, can mouses hold their breaths under water?"

"You mean can mice hold their breath?"

"Yeah, you know, when they swim under water. And dogs. Can dogs hold their breath, too?"

"Gee, I don't really know, Eric. I suppose they can close their little noses and stop breathing for a little while."

"Well, how about eagles? Are eagles big enough to carry

you on their back?"

All in all, a great afternoon. The kids had been saving up a lot of stuff to go over with Dad, and we pretty much covered the universe, although Dad was not so sure he was prepared for mouses or religion. As we pulled into the driveway, Kathryn said, "Dad, let's go to church one day."

"OK, Kathryn. Good idea. Let's talk about which one." Later that year, we attended a Passover service and a Christmas mass.

* * *

With their hearing losses, Kathryn and Eric had to work extra hard every minute of the day just to make sense of what was being said to them, using a blend of context and guesswork. They rarely complained about the tedious hearing and speech exercises. While Kathryn was compliant, Eric was more cognizant than his sister of the extra work. His complaints increased. Once, in his early elementary years, Linda asked him why the work was so hard. Eric replied, "I don't want my brain to burn up." He explained that when had to exert too much effort, he felt as if his brain was overheating.

I knew that he used his considerable mental powers to fake it, to give the impression that he knew what was going on. He wouldn't ask for clarification, because that would mean extra work. He preferred to hide his doubts rather than get into a daunting task. Over time, he acquired the ability to detect body language, take stock of context, and read lips to piece together what was being communicated. This worked to his advantage sometimes, for instance, in social settings with his friends. But in school it proved double-edged. When he didn't get a concept, he would ask for help only to discover that the help led to considerably more work. He would think that he understood what was being said, when in fact he didn't fully understand the underlying concepts.

It took time for Kathryn's large muscle coordination to catch up to her age level, but her small muscle coordination and dexterity were quite good. Eric had similar skills. Having an old Apple Lisa computer around gave them both practice in problem-solving. The kids would play video games—Oregon Trail, Pokémon, Where in the World is Carmen Sandiego?, and a half dozen others. Eric got to be very good at some of them, especially Super Mario Bros. and Donkey Kong, but too often they crowded out his schoolwork or became an escape. He was a bit of a champ around his friends. It gave him status, something he could be proud of. It was a world where he didn't have to be able to hear.

When the typing programs came out, Kathryn began to get the hang of the keyboard. One program had a little ghost, Spooky, who would hang around, floating on the screen, being patient and keeping a dialogue going, gently encouraging the player to keep typing. Kathryn went from pretty good to very good. She hit nearly 100 words a minute at one point, even taking mistakes into account. I'm a good typist and I rarely hit that mark.

That manual dexterity went together with some of her splinter skills (specialized knowledge in specific areas, like remembering a sequence of numbers). While she had a hard time with comprehension and limitations in her short-term memory, she had good working memory, for instance, she could hold arithmetic steps in her head, but couldn't remember what she did yesterday at noon. Kathryn's digit span recall was in the high normal range. "One, six, eighteen, forty-three, seven," she could easily rattle off. Then, "seven, forty-three, eighteen, six, one." At the same time, her long-term memory was as good as anybody's in our family. Kathryn is the one who never forgot birthdays or anniversaries and was always reminding us about the significant dates of family and friends. These things cheered us and sometimes made it easy to forget that the picture of Kathryn was a complicated one.

Kathryn benefited not just from the encouragement and help from Linda and me, but also from many individuals in support programs in and out of school. Special education teachers routinely gave extra help her, telling Kathryn that she could do things. Her vocabulary, nourished by teachers and people around her, showed up in her writing. Her homework was sprinkled with new words. This reinforced encouragement from teachers and helped build self-confidence in Kathryn. To top it off, Linda's attention to Kathryn's appearance and dress, plus her natural good looks and positive disposition, helped her to garner attention and win her friends.

Ironically, her positive attributes also spelled trouble for Kathryn. As she grew into her primary and middle school years, it became harder to recognize immediately that Kathryn had limitations. She presented herself effectively, as someone eagerly engaged. Her sunny, upbeat personality reinforced the image of someone focused on the speaker in small groups of friends or schoolmates, or adults for that matter. But her outward appearances masked a fog that would set in when the conversation turned the least bit abstract, or to current events, especially political and social issues that required deeper or wider knowledge.

To some extent, Eric and Kathryn both faced an unexpected disadvantage. Their outward appearance was one of sunny disposition and eager engagement. This brought the impression to newcomers and outsiders that the children were "normal." Teachers, parents, friends would assume they were more knowledgeable, more on top of things, than they actually were. This created unrealistic expectations among teachers when it came to classroom assignments, homework, and among acquaintances when it came to making friendships. It created for me also an obligation to make others aware of their limitations, and I often felt that it sounded like I was selling Kathryn and Eric short or being disingenuous, when in reality, it was just another precaution, another shadow of the Phantom falling across my fatherhood.

* * *

Despite—and perhaps because of—their limitations, I was especially proud of how the children handled themselves with adults and new acquaintances. Of all the lessons I think I ever taught my kids, the one that has proved to be the most enduring and powerful in effect is also the simplest. It goes like this:

Be sure and say thank you,

Be sure and say please.

Be sure and say excuse me, whenever you sneeze.

Be sure and use ma'am, and be sure to say sir,

Whenever you address anyone, that's for sure.

From the very beginning, I was both astounded and proud that each of the children greeting someone from any station in life exhibited equanimity and politeness. And it earned them admiring looks. Plus, those simple words—please, ma'am, and sir—seemed to lead automatically to a firm handshake and a sincere look in the eye whenever they were greeted or introduced. I was impressed with their poise when meeting grown-ups.

Years later, I learned that a good share of the credit was really due to Alana. She learned from a gifted elementary school teacher back in Berkeley that, when meeting people for the first time, "always shake with a firm grip and look them straight in the eye." One day, I'll track down Shirley from Black Pine Circle and thank her, as I thank Alana, for carrying that message forward.

Video Games Mother

One morning, when Eric was about eight, I heard a loud commotion. Eric was complaining about doing his homework with Mom. He had not had breakfast. Earlier, he was fussing with Kathryn over the Nintendo baseball game. He came into the room looking for me.

"Mom's making me do homework." He was on the verge of crying, his lip quivering. "I want to do the homework with you."

Linda came in the room. She looked as though the burden was just getting to be too much. Eric no doubt felt similarly. I could see that his defiance had taxed her last reserves. Linda had already had to cope with her own work as well as taking on Kathryn's homework. She reminded Eric about the need to follow the rules.

Learning difficulties and Eric's tendency to avoid challenges magnified the burden of homework. Every assignment needed explanation, coaching, close supervision. Linda was replicating elementary education for two kids. I played my role as well, but it was secondary to Linda's. She worked long hours with the kids even after a long day at work. I saw her as heroic in not giving up. But her capacity to stick to it far outpaced the ability of the kids to keep up, sometimes with negative results. Often, she couldn't perceive her own limits and would grow short, sometimes cross, with them. Now she was running aground with Eric.

"I've finished homework with Kathryn," Linda said. "Please speak to Eric. He's been playing video games all day."

Eric jumped up and went up to his room.

"Linda, I've been working with him most of the morning."

"He's still playing too much." Her face was drawn with emotional fatigue. "I'm going to get a timer on his video games machine," she declared. "This has got to stop."

"Linda he's only been playing twenty-five minutes. And besides, he worked hard with me on his story and workbook."

She wasn't having any argument. "He's not listening to me. I can't get him away from the monitor. He's still has to do his math homework." She was right on all counts. But Eric was out of gas.

Eric's resistance and defiance with Linda had been increasing. He had also been angry toward his sister, getting into hitting scuffles and screaming. We had hours of discussion about the difficulty Linda had with him in doing work. She had been sitting with him several days that week putting spelling words into sentences.

It didn't help for me to explain to Linda that I had words with the kids in private, to urge them to finish their work. And it didn't help when I stepped in as homework assistant with the kids. From Linda's point of view, I was never thorough enough. Looking back, I could see that we were playing out our two different models of parenting. Her instinct was to hold firm to the rules; mine was to ease them when the kids approached their limits.

Eric had started seeing a psychologist who had concluded that Eric had particular problems of writing and thinking at the same time. The psychologist urged us to get him on the computer. That helped his writing, but he did even better by simply dictating while I typed.

Linda might have agreed, but we were both so wrapped up in our battle that we didn't see our way clear to solve the problem together.

Even if I'd previously delivered the same homework message out of her hearing, Linda was unconvinced. She wanted me to say so with her in front of the kids.

"He has to hear it from his father. You have to stand up and be a man."

In the most acute clashes, Linda would play the "be a man" card. She was reacting to the failure of her own father to provide for the family when she was young. But her need collided head on with my "Not like my Dad" promise to myself. I felt the claws of a trap tighten around me. My attempt to invent my own style of fatherhood—in this case, of speaking quietly in private with the kids or doing my homework sessions, however inadequate from Linda's point of view—failed to satisfy her ideal of fatherhood.

In the middle of one such dispute, my thoughts drifted to a day recently when I had been driving Eric to school and he began to cry as we drew closer to the drop-off point. At that moment, I was deep in thought about the day ahead at work, the confrontation I was going to have with my boss over my unit's budget. Eric's quiet crying broke into my thoughts. He burst into open sobbing as we pulled into the school driveway. It was raining. I had my overcoat on. I sat with him in the back seat for half an hour, trying to get to the bottom of his upset.

I had grown to the point where I suspended whatever I was doing when I heard commotion from the homework room and went to intervene.

But when I did, Linda would say, "You have to stop undercutting me." She warned, "He needs to hear the same message from both of us." She was right, but I was conflicted. I felt that both Eric and Kathryn needed a more patient approach.

"Linda, for God's sake," I'd say. "Ease up. He's done plenty of work already. If you want him to change," I'd add in my most sincere World Bank voice, "we have to structure incentives for him. We can't just control his video time, play time, work time. He has to learn the benefits of doing that himself."

"What is it Eric?" He was whimpering and still teary. "Is it something at school?" He nodded.

"It's hard, isn't it?" His head bobbed up and down and tears dropped out in bunches. He was anxious about being in the classroom. Most of the time, he couldn't hear clearly what was going on and then had to work hard mentally to make sense of what was being said. Being there was worse than no fun; sometimes it was torture. At home, his main retreat from school was to dive into his video games. It was a world he was comfortable in.

In the confrontation with Linda, I remembered the heartache of that drop-off morning. But his mother had a point: there had to be a limit. And now, in the homework dispute, she was upping the ante with that "be-a-man" thing.

I went to the foot of the stairs and called up to his room in the deepest, most military voice I could muster.

"Eric," I said firmly. "Get down here right away." My voice had the ring of my father's. It grated on my ears. This clashed with the me I wanted to be.

"Linda, somebody needs to be a mother in this family," I said, putting a maternal arm around Eric.

"Well, somebody needs to be a father," she shot back, quietly with a defiant smile.

I was getting beaten down, no longer fighting to be the kind of father I had once dreamed about: the soft, available, confident guy, feeling strong without being like my own father. Nor had I kept my pledge to widen the spectrum of fathering skills. On the emotional front, my skills had improved, but too often I ended up feeling out of my depth. I found it easy enough to connect with the kids, but a clash with Linda set us all back. On top of that, occasionally, I had to fight off the "be a man" trope, while trying not to lose sight of where I wanted to go.

By then I had forgotten that "Yes, give her everything" vow

Linda and I had made in pediatric intensive care meant by extension that we had to be together as a whole family unit, for Kathryn and for her brother and sister. In the homework battles, I was overwhelmed by the pressures of managing our day-to-day affairs. I relied on a workaround with Linda about rules in the family. I would speak with the kids in private, to show them a lower octane version of parenting that they could trust.

Eventually, I persuaded Linda to offload the heavy burden of homework assistance to professional helpers. "No one else can mother your kids like you can," I said. She eventually saw that her mothering was more valuable than her tutoring. And I began to see that my role didn't have to be surreptitious to gain their trust in private. There was another way. Besides, financially, we were getting into a position to afford help.

Eric appeared at the head of the stairs. He was teary again, walking down slowly, anguish on his face. They were the same tears I'd seen at the school drop-off.

I felt like a fool, pressuring him when he needed under-standing and tenderness, and feeling pressured myself to take the disciplinarian fatherhood role.

Deep down, I didn't believe he needed discipline; he needed reprieve from a school routine he didn't have the tools to handle. But I had fallen for the he-man manipulation. I couldn't find the right blend—the tough love, the hard softness—and Eric was paying a price.

SALVAGING FORTY-SEVEN

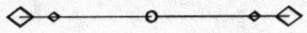

By the fall of 1990, I was still struggling to smooth out a routine in our home and my rhythm at work. The onset of a new school year and a heavy travel schedule kept me a little behind on everything. November was upon us and my forty-seventh birthday right around the corner. I needed a lift, but it seemed that a birthday wasn't going to do it. Birthdays and anniversaries had come to be a predictable, celebratory routine for the kids, but lean and minimalist for Linda and me.

Seven years earlier, I had made big plans for our fortieth birthdays (Linda and I are two months apart). For a party invitation, I drew a couple of leaping gazelles passing through a giant 0 in the number 40. My plan was to host scores of our friends. I imagined a party to match the Celebrate Life gathering we had held when Kathryn reached her first birthday. That party, where a hundred and fifty people showed up, gave us a chance to dance away our angst.

Linda buried the joint birthday party idea. "I don't want to think about it," she said. Instead, we marched forward, doing what we had to do, rarely able to escape the glimmer of lost dreams or the emotional cacophony of daily life.

Turning forty-seven was a lifetime removed from that birthday wish seven years earlier. Berkeley had receded to a distant memory, replaced by the frantic pace of the World Bank and home life in Chevy Chase. I knew by then that it was going to be a long time before I got back to Berkeley, but I kept the dream alive. Maybe that's why I longed so much for a birthday party on my forty-seventh. Candles, cake, ice cream, singing and presents were almost always a part of celebration at birthdays, except for one time.

I had missed Alana's twelfth birthday months earlier that same year. And by missed, I don't mean I was traveling. I mean her birthday came and went without the smallest acknowledgement on my part. Distractions from work, therapies, household repairs after a heavy snow, a hundred reasons for losing sight of her birthday, none of them acceptable. I discovered the error a week later and felt miserable. I just simply blew it. It left me feeling empty and a failure, having let her down at such a critical time, when she was being so independent, trying to complete a transition from West Coast to East. Right when she most needed a flourish or two, Alana got the short end of the stick. She told me years later that she had no recollection of that transgression, but it still hangs there in my closet of bad deeds.

* * *

Missing her birthday reminded me of the only other complete whiff on an easy, softball slow pitch that should have been a knock-out-of-the-park reward: a tooth fairy lapse when she was six.

"Daddy, I put my tooth under the pillow, but the fairy didn't come!" Alana had exclaimed, innocently, when she came downstairs for breakfast. She wore a mournful expression.

"What?" I said loudly in fake surprise, doing my best to conceal my utter failure.

"Are you sure?" I mounted a flourish and a fallback plan all in one grand gesture. "Let's go look again."

Before she could answer, I raced upstairs jamming my hand in my pants pocket where I kept my money. I fumbled blindly for a couple of dollars as I raced up the stairs, being sure to stay well ahead of Alana. I dashed into her room and stuffed the bills under her pillow.

"Alana," I called out as she entered the room. "Come here and look a little more carefully." My plan worked. Full offense, no equivocation. She ran past me and lifted the pillow.

"Wow, Daddy. Look!" she exclaimed, reaching down to clutch the bills. "Twenty-five dollars!"

"Alana," I said with wide eyes. There was no going back. "The fairy must have thought you were being an extra good sister."

* * *

Except for the one missed birthday, the kids' celebrations always included the goodies of cake, candles, and ice cream, shared in a family circle with singing. For Linda and me, it took a little more energy and, most of the time, some reminding and urging from the kids. Our self-celebratory spirit had been gradually worn down by the steady winds of special needs.

Linda awoke on the twenty-fourth, my birthday, completely forgetting that it was my day. She had strep throat and was immobilized. "I feel awful," she said. "You'll have to take over today."

I spent that Saturday in my Land's End warm-ups, like a uniformed driver, chauffeuring kids to the pediatrician for their sore throats, to the puppet show, to the movies. By the time I picked up Alana after the movies, I had completely lost track of that small star of hope, the one to remind me at least that growing old came with a small degree of wisdom, a pat on the back. I didn't want a party or gifts. I just wanted a little glimmer of recognition, something to make the day stand out, to have a little more color, a tad more warmth. I would even have settled for false respect. Forget festive.

"Dad, can you take us shopping?" Alana asked, when I picked her up from movies with her friends. We went to the mall where she was to meet up with her boyfriend (her first—at least the first one she introduced to me). She had been careful to keep him at a distance from the family. He was born into the new wealth of the Potomac set, where the strong scent of money wafts through the neighborhoods. He seemed to have been inoculated from the usual spoiling of rich kids by guilty, absentee parents. He stood up from his chair as I approached their table. As he rose, I was struck by the second or two it took him to rise to his full height. At thirteen, he was already a half-foot taller than I was. I looked up to him. He offered his hand. "How do you do, Mr. Campbell," he said, politely. Alana beamed next to him. I felt her growing too, zooming up in stature and confidence if not in inches.

Alana had been straining to break out on her own. Being accepted in the Potomac environment went hand in hand with her growing independence. I feared that she was smarting from the contrast she saw between our lifestyle and that of her friends in big, modern-day mansions. I feared that she didn't want to invite her friends to our house in Chevy Chase, afraid that she thought it was too suburban, too "valley," no matter the five mortgages and a million dollars in real estate. In reality, I was projecting my own inadequacy onto her. She was growing up. It was I who was struggling, I who needed the comforting.

These projections reminded me of my own sense of shame at my humble circumstances growing up. I used to wonder why my father couldn't join the honorary sheriff's posse in Sacramento, like my friends' fathers did, and ride in the warm summer nights on one of those magnificent golden palominos in formation with silver-studded saddles and fluttering flags. Those riders—building contractors, accountants, and bar owners—looked so proud and on top of the world. We lived in a small four-room house on the edge of town. Dad had one foot on his miniature, make-believe farm of two acres and, by that time, the other foot in a white-collar world, a commercial bank where he had made a transition from government bureaucrat to commercial lending in agri-business.

No amount of storytelling to Alana about my college-era pledge to forgo wealth—that "it's not about money in life"—could bend her in a direction away from the one I feared she was taking. I tried many ways to explain my values, to tell the tales of working as laborer in hop fields and summertime construction. It didn't seem to make much of an impression. Neither did Peace Corps stories about living in poverty trying to make a better world. None of that seemed to make a dent in her preferences for the glittery Potomac set. Our circumstances in Chevy Chase fell well short of the miniature estates sitting cheek by jowl in that neighborhood of fast risers. I felt that my ensemble of values didn't have the appeal for her that I had hoped. I learned years later that I was way wrong, that my worries in 1990 were completely unfounded. My disappointment at the time reflected my own sense of not measuring up.

At the end of the day, I sat in my room, tired and alone, the kids off with friends, Linda ill. I held out hope that someone would still remember. I was too proud to remind anybody. Should I give in to my urge to weep? Was there any hope in overcoming these headwinds, pushing me back into older age, into a losing battle of intergenerational values? Being forgotten on my birthday.

Starting the car made me feel better. I launched a one-man salvation mission. I beat it down the road to Sam Goody's. Two years in that town, and I had never even blown a few crisp twenties on music cassettes. No matter that the technology was practically obsolete already. How long can tapes stand up to those polished hard CDs? The store featured a whole shelf of fifties and sixties tunes, just right for reminiscence. Comfort music. Top hits for every year from 1955. Martha and the Vandellas, Roy Orbison, Percy Sledge. Why not load up? Would Alana ever believe, much less accept, this music from way before her time?

Motown blasted away on the car stereo as I hurtled down

Wisconsin Avenue for champagne from that one liquor store that still might be open after nine p.m. California Safeways, open twenty-four hours, will sell you sixteen labels of cabernets and ten of champagnes. Store owners in Bethesda, on the other hand, had closed shop and by nightfall on Saturday, were getting their clothes ready for church the next morning.

I found a cheap bottle of Brut Dargent. Champagne, music, and a few laughs with my friend, Lionel—that could rescue the day. But no luck, his house was dark. He had gone to bed early in preparation for travel the following day. My small crusade for independence and reconstruction of celebration ended in failure. One hundred and fifty at the Celebrate Life; zero at forty-seven.

I wasn't going to give up without salvaging something, though. Improvising at the wheel, I nipped into Uno's Pizza. Musing and daydreams at the bar while I waited for a Chicago's Original. Then, home at last with a tidy pizza box and some still cold Brut Dargent on the seat.

I walked in the door a few minutes to ten, a little more than two hours to go before the magic day would end. Kathryn, then nine, came running in with Eric, six, meeting me with wild eyes and giggles.

"Daddy, Daddy, happy birthday, Daddy!" they exclaimed, rushing over, arms wide-open for hugs.

"Dad, we have been wrapping presents," they shouted out gleefully. Small packages wrapped in newspaper with scotch tape were paraded in and placed on the table. And yes, there was cake, Sarah Lee, still in the carton, several pieces missing. Linda stood pale and disheveled behind the kids.

The party was impromptu, but it was there, enough to crowd out my depressing confrontation with Alana, enough to resuscitate the memory of turning forty, enough for another decade. The champagne cork shot out with a blast. Linda handed me the cake knife. "Happy forty-sev-enth," she whispered softly. Alana chimed in, eyes glistening, "Happy birthday, Daddy."

My family salvaged forty-seven in more ways than they knew. Looking back now, my brief interlude of self-pity afforded me important moments of reflection, even grief, about all that had happened in the preceding decade. I got back in touch with the loss of my father and the loss of Kathryn's life as a healthy child. I meditated about survival, about plugging forward, and about milestones like forty-seven, my most memorable birthday of all.

SPIN AND ROLL

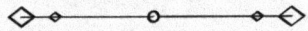

We rode in our Ford Aerostar, a van I had modified for family travel, headed south on Highway 17 to visit Linda's mother for the Christmas holiday in 1990. Taking out half the backseat made room to lie down on long trips like this one to Florida. Bifurcating the van also reflected the parenting schism developing between Linda and me. I lay in the back with Kathryn, Alana rode on pillows behind the driver's seat, Linda drove, Eric played word games in the passenger seat. We rumbled together along the highway ahead of a summer rainstorm.

Something awakened me from dozing.

With my ear so close to the floorboards, I heard and felt a change in tone—from a droning rumble on the highway to a softened skid—and knew that grass, not pavement, was beneath our wheels. I could see only the sky from below the windows in my supine position. The onset of a soft rumble came with a peculiar feel. Our momentum forward shifted to an inertial movement sideways, and I realized we were off the highway and starting to spin. The wheels raked over the grass until we came about a full 360 degrees. We started to tip. A storm of luggage, sleeping bags, beach equipment, clothes, toys, books—all our vacation stuff came raining down on Kathryn and me as the van turned upside down. Now the storm was inside the van.

Kathryn's eyes sprang open. She clung to me with a frozen stare as we waited for the spin to end. It had taken us back up onto the highway. The roll played itself out, putting us wrong side up, back in the fast lane. When we came to rest, buried in belongings and still lying down, I glanced through the back window to see a long caravan of oncoming traffic, weaving to and fro as drivers braked and swerved to arrest their forward motion lest they crash into us. I tensed, petrified and trapped. If they didn't stop, it would be the end. Fortunately, the spectacle of our spin and roll on the wide grassy median gave them ample time to avoid hitting us.

"Kathryn, are you OK?" I asked, looking down at her, both of us still lying on the inside roof panel, covered with belongings.

Kathryn looked up, fright plastered on her face, but no tears. She knew how to take comfort. Someone was always there trying to hold up the sky for her, but this time it wasn't me. Someone held up the sky for both of us that day. Neither of us was hurt.

Through a side window, I caught sight of Alana, fifteen, already out of the car with Linda and Eric, then eight. They stood on the median between the north- and southbound lanes, looking expectantly at the van. Alana was taking tentative steps toward the upside-down wreckage. She had escaped unharmed and realized that her dad and sister were still inside. With a look of great distress, she called out "Daddy! Daddy?"

That was a moment that seared me deep inside, my daughter's voice crying out in fear and desperation. It was like an echo from the past. I had cried out from the beginning of Kathryn's illness a decade earlier and had cried out in a very different, muted way, when I had to tell Alana that her grandfather had died the night Kathryn had survived multiple heart failures. My answer back to her was an affirmation of the present.

"We're OK, Alana," I shouted, hoping she could hear me through the walls of the van.

A motorist walked up to the van and opened the rear hatch, which crashed down to the pavement. I pulled Kathryn out with me and made our way over to Linda, Alana, and Eric, huddling together on the grass. They were in a daze, standing exposed to a soft rain and the rapidly cooling afternoon.

Linda's face was twisted with guilt. She looked as though she had just burned down the house. A quick survey confirmed that everyone was OK. I picked up Eric. Linda put her arms around Alana and Kathryn.

"Wow, E," I said, trying to allay his fears, "you just came through a big wreck, and look at you. Not a scratch."

"Yeah, Dad," he mumbled. "What happened?"

"You tell me, big guy. How did you get out of your seat belt?"

"Easy. When I saw we were going off the road, I just slid down under the seat." He had a look of pride on his face. "I was doing my puzzle game," he continued. "Mom told me that I made a wrong move. Then we started to spin."

Linda shrank back.

"You OK?" I said, turning to Linda.

"Trembling. Not a scratch."

I gave Linda the burn look. An image of the Phantom sprang to mind, flashing a warning about Linda just as he had warned me about my dad. Glancing at Eric's word puzzle while driving sixty-five in the fast lane, she'd then drifted into soft gravel at the edge of the road. Her belt kept her from a bad throw-down.

I felt an impulse of anger crop up toward Linda, a new fissure in the gulf already separating our relationship.

"And you, Alana. Last time I checked, you were on your knees right behind Mom. What did you do?"

"I just put my hands up on the roof and did a cartwheel as we went over." She beamed. Just like Alana. Managing through the mess of our family and coming out on her feet. The spin and roll, a near catastrophe, left our van and our vacation in tatters, but the kids were unscathed. They'd made the right moves in time of crisis.

A kind motorist pulled up on the grass. "Get in," the guy said. "It's getting colder. You can wait in here where it's warm until the tow truck comes."

Kathryn elected to come with me in the tow truck while the Good Samaritan drove the others to a local motel. We rode in silence to a car rental place outside Savannah, just across the state line.

"Give me the biggest car you've got," I said to the rental guy. "We had an accident, and I need to feel safe."

"Happens every time," the agent said. "After an accident, they always want the biggest."

Driving back north to the motel, Kathryn was showing signs of breaking out of her always-compliant mode, stepping into new territory of self-awareness. She was dwarfed by the front seat of the giant sedan. A tiny contradiction, she was still a little gangly in her pre-adolescence, yet with an adult pose, her legs crossed. We rode in silence for a while. She seemed to have grown up over the last couple of hours.

"Dad," she started. "It's about your wife."

"Yeah?" I asked. "What do you mean, my wife?"

"It's about your wife. You know, Linda." Kathryn paused. "She's part of the problem."

"Yes, Kathryn." I smiled inside. "You know, we all have our problems."

She was gaining just enough understanding to see that Mom and Dad weren't entirely on the same page. Dad, the always softie compared to her mom, made it easier for Kathryn to see fault in Linda. Beyond the spin and role, Kathryn perceived that neither of her parents were entirely comfortable with their spouse's take on parenting, nor entirely comfortable with their own take. She still didn't know how lost her parents really were.

Kathryn and I returned to find the family huddled together, warming, calming down. I gazed out on the sylvan plain of South Carolina, graceful sea pines ringing my view, and thought about the wreck of our van sitting upside down in a snarl of traffic.

GAMES WE PLAYED

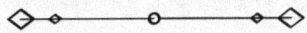

Early in the fatherhood project, I saw sports and physical activities as a retreat from the tensions of managing disabilities, just as organized sports had been an escape from domestic storms with my dad. I enjoyed sports before and during high school. I intended to get my kids involved in athletics and games, both for teaching rules and fair play, and to offer respite from the work of parenting. I was wrong on both counts. Rulemaking proved to be as complicated, and fair play as elusive in our games as they were in everyday life.

Like most suburban parents, we signed the kids up for team sports early and year-round. Though Linda could glide gracefully down any ski slope, her strong suit was finding sports classes, courses, games, and instructors. For Alana, sports were just another opportunity to express her natural organizational as well as athletic gifts. She was in the thick of it as athlete or manager in gymnastics, tennis, and swimming.

Kathryn was in a category by herself. Comprehending the big picture—understanding the mechanics of the game, grasping her responsibilities, and figuring out her positioning—was a challenge for her. In the best of times, it was amusing to watch Kathryn and her soccer teammates. At one moment running in a small herd after the ball, the next they would be standing in the group discussing fingernail polish and tightening ponytails while the action went on elsewhere.

Positioning on the field was a major challenge. While her teammates got the hang of their positions in the field, Kathryn often ran aimlessly, still pretty much clueless about where to be. Then one day, out of the blue on a wide soccer pitch, Kathryn, positioned as a defender, made a sharp, nearly involuntary jab at the ball as an offensive player went sweeping by, and the ball came dislodged. It plopped down in front of Kathryn. She instinctively bolted forward and had the entire pitch out in front of her. She dribbled the length of the field. No one was going to catch her. Those of us standing on the sideline erupted into a coordinated cheer. Everyone recognized the breakthrough moment for Kathryn after three years of scoreless playing. But could she drive it home? She reached the front of the penalty box at the far end of the field, made a slight head fake, something no one had taught her to do, and nudged the ball forward into the net for her first score.

I fell flat on my back on the grass in tears, hoarse from cheering. The other parents circled around patting and clapping, congratulating me on Kathryn's success, her teammates celebrating Kathryn. She hardly knew how to handle the accolades of her teammates. No one was more surprised at her feat than Kathryn herself.

She liked the taste of scoring and began to post more points as her nose for the game sharpened. She found herself standing around the goal. When the ball would pop free or ricochet off, she would put it in. The lifting feeling came with a jolt of pride. But for me, there was something extra. Kathryn was doing things "normal" kids did. She was succeeding. The moisture of self-confidence made her life a little greener after what seemed like a century of drought.

* * *

Eric had the same athletic gifts as his siblings, but they didn't appear immediately and only blossomed during his teen years. In his very first day of soccer for five-year-olds, Eric somehow ended up as goalie, and within minutes of the first session on the pitch, he faced a concerted if innocent attack. The boys understood immediately that offense consisted of getting the ball in the net, and defense, led by Eric, was to keep it out. A gaggle of boys eagerly chased the ball into the goalie box where Eric immediately dove upon it, smothering it with his body. He was a natural. But the impromptu stampede carried a half dozen boys in a cloud of dust kicking awkwardly at the ball even as it lay under Eric's curled up body.

The coach was quick to the rescue, pulling Eric free from the overly enthusiastic scrum. I stood nearby, petrified by conflicting emotions. One pushed me forward to fend off the on-rushing players and protect Eric; the other demanded I stay back, to observe a blurry line, to allow Eric to survive the attack and feel the achievement of having done his job well.

The tension broke when the coach, standing only a few feet away, lifted Eric to daylight still clutching the ball, his hair and face covered with dust, his teeth clenched. The coach raised his voice, signaling an immediate end to the siege. The boys settled back and fell into a calm, their faces slowly turning from the excitement of stampede to the grudging admiration of Eric, now standing, holding the ball, having saved the goal.

I joined in celebrating Eric for his bravery—a primitive reaction coming out full-blown in my five-year-old—embracing him with praise and encouragement. But I recognized immediately that forays into sport weren't always going to be like a pleasant run on a soft, sunny, pitch.

Like soccer, baseball came naturally, if not easily, for Eric. I felt somehow in a better position to help in baseball, since it had been my own sport as well. As he grew older and more competent, I felt a palpable urge—related to my father's ambivalence about my success in sports—to help Eric to succeed.

One Saturday afternoon in the summer of 1991, I sat on the edge of the bench behind the backstop, leaning forward and encouraging Eric to take some practice swings as a pitcher was about to deliver.

"Step in, Eric," I said softly, as the pitcher reared back to throw. Eric was within earshot, but, because his hearing aids were pinched in underneath his helmet, I wasn't sure that he could hear me. (He told me years later that he could not.) I called out more than stage whispered, "Remember to start your step when he makes his kick." I did my best to give him a minute-by-minute, second-by-second management. Eric fouled off the first pitch.

"Good job Eric, way to get around," I said again softly. I didn't notice the side glances given to me by the other dad coaches in the area. I saw myself as the opposite of the absentee dad, perhaps compensating for the times when I, like my father, was MIA while traveling. During his at-bats, I would be there, the quiet narrator but in overdrive, earnestly offering batting wisdom in real time.

I didn't fully appreciate the degree to which I was overstepping my fatherly coaching responsibilities until the next season. The coach announced matter-of-factly to the three or four of us dads engaged with the team, that this year there would be no more talking to the players while they're playing. The announcement hit me with a heavy thud. I looked around. The other dads just kept their eyes straight ahead or at their feet. It was clear it was aimed at me. I took it as the friendly advice that it was. But I saw how far over the line I had gone. I throttled back after that. I needed to find a quieter, less intrusive way to support Eric or get out of the way altogether.

* * *

"OK, you guys, Nerf-ball time," I would announce, to get a game going on a rainy evening or quiet weekend. The two little ones would come running into the bedroom, eager to play. Kathryn and Eric would take turns catching the Nerf football pass from Dad.

I invented Nerf-ball catch as a way to be engaged with the kids, to help them with physical activity, to teach, but most of all so that the kids, mainly Eric and Kathryn, could play together. So many other games—table games, guessing games and the like—left Kathryn at a disadvantage. A psychiatrist friend of the family once pointed out that, speaking in terms of intellect, our kids were separated by four standard deviations, meaning that IQs ran from below average to the top one percent. Nerf-ball was one small way to bridge that gulf. Also, it worked well as a joint activity—indoors, on rainy days or at night, even though, on occasion, yes, we broke a lamp or two.

Our Nerf-ball game also had the advantage of flexible rules. I could manipulate rules on the spot to level the playing field.

"Remember, two points at chest hight, three points for over the head or out wide, four points for a diving catch on the bed." They pushed and giggled, jostling to get in front for the first throw.

"OK, let's pick a rule for who goes first."

"The date rule, the date rule," cried Eric. He knew he was born on an odd day, Kathryn on an even.

"OK, today's the thirteenth, so it's you first, Eric." Kathryn pouted and stammered, but the rule worked well enough half the time for her.

The kids grew adept at snagging the soft Nerf ball, even when I put some zip on it. Diving onto the bed was harder for Kathryn. She was pretty nimble but didn't have the soft hands Eric did. Although her muscle tone had improved compared to her early toddler years, her eye-hand coordination wasn't as good as Eric's. She would invariably lose on points. She would sink into a puddle trying to keep up. I fell into that no-man's land where the legacy of heartache pushed me to make it better. Bend the rules.

"OK, Kathryn, you get one extra-credit try." She would brighten a bit; Eric would frown. That was the improvisation that poisoned my rulemaking. I could feel the little tear in my heart every time she struggled, another tear when Eric fussed, or vice versa. That's when my dad would have done better. Draw the line, keep it there. Resist that urge to hold up the sky at every turn.

Roller ball, a game we played on the beach, was less amenable to rule-bending. We dug a target hole in the sand big enough for a tennis ball to fall in. Each of us taking turns would stand behind a line in the sand drawn five or six yards from the hole and try to sink a "putt" as we rolled the ball underhand toward the target. The kids were no less competitive, and they would squeal and shout with glee with each successful toss. This game didn't have the rocky endings of catching the Nerf ball, even though sometimes a second chance, occasionally a third, would be allow all players a chance to overcome yawning disparities in scores.

Extra chances at games were a concomitant of extra explanations about everything else, for instance, what the plan for the day was, what time we leave, what time we come back. How many times did I hold up the troupe—suspend action at the beach, on picnics, in the car—to explain to Kathryn what was next, why we were stopping here or there. These things were repeated many times, but Kathryn always needed extra reminders and a fuller explanation. Eric grew frustrated having to wait while his sister caught up. I prided myself on maintaining patience with her, but now think I should have tried harder to get around the problems of memory and preparedness, perhaps by writing them down, or asking her to internalize them more deliberately, instead of being on call. Electronic personal assistants and smart phones worked well for those purposes, but they came too late to help Kathryn before she was ten.

"Why can't I go up the chair lift with you guys?" she complained.

"Kathryn, you have to get your skis under you first, get your balance and be confident on the snow." Kathryn frowned. She was turning eleven and just starting on the snow. Alana and Eric were already whizzes, schussing down the mountains like pros.

I took her hand. "Come over to the rope tow, Kathryn. That's where you start."

Kathryn had terrible difficulty finding her balance on her skis while holding onto the rope. I spent several afternoons on the bunny hill and rope tow, a line that hauled skiers up 150 yards to a leveled mound where they could let go of the rope and practice skiing down a gentle slope. But the bouncing tension in the rope, the fits and starts of the pull, and the icy tracks in the path, all conspired to throw skiers off balance. Time after time, Kathryn would grab on, make it a few yards and only to let go of the rope before falling.

With each fall, I would trudge up the snow, pull her up and out of the way of the skiers behind her, and start over again at the bottom. "Kathryn. You have to hold on to the rope, tight," I admonished her. An overflow of anger, long pent up, crowded out my patience, putting a curtness on my words. I was tired of being a saint, tired of aiming to be the patient dad, yet I knew that to show anger and frustration would impose emotional obstacles for her. I desperately wanted her to be with the family, to enjoy our outings together.

"OK, here you go. Get your skis under you. That's it." I positioned Kathryn in a straight-ahead alignment. "Remember, hold on tight, no matter what."

At last, in the waning hours of the afternoon, Kathryn got past ten yards. She held on. "Hold on, Kathryn, hold on!" I hollered, running up behind her as she pulled away up the hill under rope power. A surge of exhilaration pulsed inside me. I could see her hunching over, her muscles tightening, her butt sticking out, one ski trailing off to one side only to be corrected. She was struggling to hold her balance but keeping it and making it further up the hill.

"Hold ooonnnnn!" I called out one last time, whooping, running up behind her.

By this time, adults and children standing around were cheering and clapping for Kathryn. They had witnessed her many tries over the course of the day. She began to crest the hill, reaching the top of the gate where the hill flattened out on the turnaround platform. A crowd of young skiers were standing there watching Kathryn succeed.

Kathryn crossed the flat turnaround area. I celebrated, shouting with arms in the air.

But she did not let go of the rope at the turnaround. She did not to let go of that damn rope, and she was pulled right up through the gate, broke through yellow tape surrounding the area, and disappeared in the trees behind the turnaround zone still holding the rope.

I raced up the hill, wading through snow, laughing and hollering, whooping in excitement. I found her sitting in the snow, beaming with delight. We laughed together and celebrated her successful run. It was working at last.

Some months later during the same winter in the beginning of 1992, we returned to the mountain for another family ski. Kathryn had advanced to a two-person chair and now, with sister Alana, we were about to try a three-person chairlift. We shuffled forward in the line of skiers waiting to be picked up. Their colorful clothing and equipment formed a life-sized chain, like a colorful string of DNA on the mountain. It was a beautiful day in the Tahoe Valley, the lake shimmering far below, the snow perfect for skiing.

Linda and I took turns skiing with the kids. On this day, she skied with Eric. I relished the opportunity to be on the slopes with my two daughters, to take on a new challenge, the three of us more or less on equal terms. Alana was by now ready for black diamond (advanced) runs. I wasn't as strong a skier as Alana, but able to stay in shouting distance and to keep sight of Kathryn. Waiting for her to complete her run and catch up to us didn't have the tedium we'd felt in the past. On this hill, she was beginning to catch up.

However, the three-person lift presented a new challenge. Our previous rides up the slopes had been on a double. Kathryn had become proficient at that, though it took some walking and talking her through it. She would need more on the three-person lift.

"Kathryn, stay close to me on my right side."

She had sidestepped her way over and fell against my leg. "You got it there, honey? You OK?"

"Uh-huh," she grunted, a little frustrated with the awkward leverage of skis.

A giant wheel at the base of the lift lay on its side, turning quietly, conveying the thick cable from which the wide, three-person benches were suspended.

"Now, watch those guys in front of us. See how they line up and turn to the outside to reach the chairlift as it comes around?" We watched several trios in front of us manage the coordination as they were skimmed away into the air.

"When the chair comes around, just sit down with me. I'll be in the middle to help." In fact, it was a mistake for me to be in the middle. It would have been easier for Kathryn to be there or on the inside where the lift moved more slowly as it made the turn. But for reasons of weight distribution, the lift attendants had that heaviest-in-the-center rule.

"OK," she said, a little fidgety and nervous. After all, it had only been a couple of months since she had mastered the tow rope up the bunny hill. I still chuckled at the memory of her plowing through the yellow tape and up into the trees. Now she was skiing comfortably and able to keep herself under control.

"We're next!" Alana shouted.

"OK, Kathryn, as soon as these guys in front of us move away, shuffle into position with your skis on the blue line, see?"

"Uh-huh. That blurry one, there?" she pointed to the line

under the snow in the middle of the loading platform. "That one?"

"That's right, that's the one." There was only one. "Just move calmly to that spot, line up with Alana and me."

The chairlift came swinging around and whisked away the trio in front of us.

"OK, here we go," I said. I moved quickly, helping Kathryn onto the loading platform. Alana moved expertly right into position. We lined up with the blue painted line under our skis.

Our anxiety built up knowing that we would have only a few seconds to be in sync. Five hundred pairs of eyes were watching. Maybe Kathryn wasn't the most nervous person around. "Kathryn, keep your skis right on this line." She edged in and found her position.

The chair came swinging around and slowed automatically for us to take our sitting positions. At that moment, Kathryn edged backward to meet the chair. She moved too soon, as if to sit early and in doing so, she bumped the chair.

"Kathryn, no!" I said, in a muted shout.

Her small collision with the chair caused it to angle off to one side toward Alana, and it clipped Alana early, throwing her off balance. As the chair accelerated away, all three of us were only partly on the chairlift.

The ground fell quickly from beneath us. I had slid down nearly to the small of my back on the lift. Our awkward loading happened too fast to even utter a word. I dropped my poles and threw my arms out, catching Kathryn around the waist with my right arm and Alana with my left. Both girls were perched precariously, more off than on the chair, our legs dangling over the edge as we pulled into the air, our altitude rising to ten, fifteen, eighteen feet in a matter of seconds. I mustered every ounce of strength I had to grasp the chair frame and wriggle my butt back up onto the lip of the chair, grunting. The girls were petrified, barely able to emit a sound. I torqued first left then right to get Kathryn back up; Alana was out of danger and getting herself back into sitting position.

It was a frightening moment. We were thirty-five or forty feet off the ground by the time we were settled. It was a moment that captured in vivid miniature the discoordination in the family. Kathryn's small movement, made out of sync with others, had out-sized effects. And yeah, I saved them, and the kids thought I was a hero. But I had caused the problem in the first place. On the chair, I should have positioned the kids in a way that would have made it easier for Kathryn. The fumbling hand of a wannabe savior—hero and goat in one fell swoop.

* * *

On the subsequent ski trip, Alana and I had a moment together. It was another glorious day. We were alone for the first time in months, while Linda skied with Kathryn and Eric. That afternoon was a time for us to catch up on some one-on-one after so much turbulence and hurry, always playing catch-up, trying to stay ahead of the family's entropic tumble. Alana reminded me of our trip to explore under the

Golden Gate. We chuckled about the car with the airplane. We spoke of her school and friends. The quiet solitude and warm camaraderie were enhanced by the fabulous perspective high over the Tahoe Valley, a perspective that lifted us away from the troubled times of the recent past. We dismounted the chairlift and skied a short distance before stopping to take in the view. We shared a Snickers bar, giggling.

That was when I caught sight of a red blur moving impossibly fast toward us. Out of the corner of my eye came a flash, a bright red parka. He whizzed by so fast and so close that my heart leapt. His skis literally went over the back of Alana's skis.

"You fucker!" I muttered. He could've killed us both. His partner went howling down the hill after him, laughing and shouting. "Hotdogs" is too kind a word for those guys. Today, they would've been thrown off the mountain.

But back then, it was left for us to deal with it. Alana and I were shaken and bummed out. She was on the verge of tears. We made our way back to the ski lift and took the next chair going down the mountain. Halfway down, we caught site of the red and blue parkas coming up on the lift, and they saw us. We glared as we passed them. They let out loud laughs and catcalls. That was the last time I skied on that Tahoe mountain. Alana was back the next day and continued to get better.

* * *

Later in the same year, I found myself having to invent a very different kind of game. I came home one afternoon and found Kathryn's pet fish, Charlie, vertical in his little tank, his open mouth hanging from the surface of the water. My distress surprised me. The little fish's position was similar to Kathryn's a decade earlier, when Linda had first detected that our newborn was in heart failure. She had handed me Kathryn; I'd held her vertical, her head back, her mouth open, gasping for air. My insides turned over, the sight of the little fish recalling the bewilderment and helplessness, the panic that I had felt while holding infant Kathryn. A small fish in a small tank. That's how thin my emotional ice was then, moved to tears by the sight of a tiny creature dying.

And then there was the question of how to break this news to Kathryn. She had no concept of death, of mortality, of the finite nature of life. At age eleven, Kathryn's knowledge base hinged on the immediate, the concrete. She knew games, sports, direct relationships. But she hadn't contemplated the meaning of life and the universe, the finality of death.

My instinct—the holding-up-the-sky instinct—was to protect her from this small confrontation with death. I didn't know what else to do. I wasn't ready for that larger conversation. Her own mortality was still too close, too raw. In retrospect, it was a perfect time to engage the question, but I wasn't prepared to deal with it. I needed somehow to first bring her—and me—fully into a world of living.

I dashed out of the house and drove to the variety store where I had seen little toy fish, wooden figures all painted in tropical colors almost the size of Kathryn's fish. I purchased two or three.

"Cute," the clerk said. "Are you going to put them on a window sill.?"

"No," I said, "in a bowl," and ran out.

I disposed of the dead fish, cleaned out the bowl, laid new gravel in the bottom and placed the little wooden fish on the gravel. It looked passably like the real thing. I hoped Kathryn wouldn't notice my pathetic cover-up. Because of her memory issues—for instance, forgetting to feed the fish—several days had passed before Kathryn discovered the truth. But her reaction surprised me.

"Dad, what happened to Charlie?"

I met Kathryn's gaze and paused a few seconds and then said. "Kathryn, Charlie is gone, but this new fish will never die." Kathryn looked quizzically at me. Tears begin to form in her eyes.

"Charlie is not coming back?"

"No, Kathryn, Charlie is not coming back. Charlie's dead." I paused. "I thought this little symbol of a fish would help soften the blow, to remember Charlie by." Kathryn was weeping softly. "When you are ready, we will get another Charlie."

We hugged quietly for a long time.

* * *

While Linda shared a passion and proficiency skiing with the kids, I aimed to engage the children more directly in celebrations of first goals and small achievements with our ball games. In all the games we played, there came moments of compensation, extra time, personal accommodation, even when it came to clumsy camouflage of dead pets. Making up games had the advantage of engaging in joint activities, but the disadvantage of forcing competition in an inherently uneven playing field. I was still cutting my teeth in the hybrid model of a father. I now realize that something else was happening that I didn't appreciate or catch onto fast enough.

For one thing, the purest form of playing—making ordinary tasks more fun, pulling in a lightness to our lives, remembering the larger arc of living—was more important than games themselves. Yes, there were chores, homework and difficult tasks, but they didn't have to be dolorous, as Kathryn would say. Inwardly, I played a defensive game too much of the time. I didn't admit it openly, but I quietly readied myself for something to go wrong, tried too hard, even in calm situations like excessive coaching, instead of letting them learn it on their own because I was so worried that they wouldn't or couldn't keep up with their peers.

Still, games and an attitude of free play strengthened the children's attachment to Linda and me and us to them. That bonding led to a tissue of trust that grew over the years.

As the kids grew older and met the challenge of new adventures in games, the ground shifted beneath me. They were growing stronger by small degrees, as I was searching an ever-shifting comfort zone in fathering. I dimly perceived that sky-holding—that Phantom instinct to protect, to be aggressive, or to shut down aggression—was no longer the main task. I wasn't ready for that moment with the fish but I probably did not have to fret. I overdid it in coaching in baseball and patience with Kathryn. In the end, they were moving faster than I was. Every step of the way, in sports, games, life, they were more capable of fending for themselves than I gave them credit for.

BREAKING AND FIXING

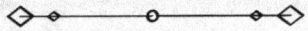

O ne afternoon in the late fall of 1995, the upstairs tub started to leak, so I tore out the ceiling and immediately felt better. The water didn't stop, but action was taken. I tended to break up my to-do list into small bits. It wasn't just fix the upstairs leak. The list read, "1. demo the wall, 2. check for source." The third item read: "3. develop options to repair the leak." The job was to stop the leak. But just with "demo" I could show progress. It was my way of recording the advance. Checking something off the list made me feel better.

Things Fall Apart

I crashed my way through lath and plaster like an expert, found the leak, and took a break, contemplating my progress. My children were very impressed. The little ones peered up from below my perch on the ladder.

"How did you learn to do that, Dad?" one asked, standing amidst a pile of rubble.

Blowing dust and small debris off my arm, I replied, "Lots of practice."

They looked at the exposed beams and piles of sheet rock

and lath, nodded their heads, and walked out reverently. That's right, there's their father, straightening out the world.

I didn't tell them that my quick fix two months ago to cover the missing escutcheon around the tub spout actually helped clog the flow of water in the first place, forcing it into the cracks in the splash wall, down behind the tile, to pool silently under the tub and directly over the entry hall ceiling downstairs where I was now standing on the ladder. The pool had sat there waiting until the pressure of a body in the tub pushed it through the ceiling.

The pressure came from Alana taking a soak after the doctor had discovered a cyst, and told her that she needed to soak. As soon as she sat in the tub, the water began to pour through the ceiling.

The ceiling I could repair. Most of the other stuff in life, I couldn't. I could only cope, manage, sometimes postpone. But fix? That was a bridge too far.

In this case, Alana needed the tub, so I swung into action. Had it not been for the cyst, the leak would have gone unnoticed for, who knows? Maybe for months.

When the water had started spurting out of the ceiling, Linda came running upstairs in a panic. She happened to be looking at mail in the entry hall when the flood started. She ran right past the gushing water and up the stairs to tell me about the leak, which I could hear easily from my spot on the second floor. I didn't let on to anyone about my culpability in the leak. I did intend to take the credit for fixing it. Now I stared at the gaping hole in the ceiling. Looked like it had taken a direct hit from a bowling ball.

Mending Our Lives

Leaking tubs and old pipes were the least of the things that contributed to the entropy in our household. Kathryn's memory and comprehension issues and Eric's auditory processing and executive function problems, as well as their hearing disorders, outpaced my best efforts to maintain order. Things would get lost or be forgotten or misunderstood. It wasn't just hearing aids in junipers or batteries that fell into obscure places.

One day, Kathryn placed our adorable Bichon Frise, Belle, high up on a bookshelf in her room where she thought she could keep an eye on her. She then had to go to the bathroom, and completely forgot about putting the dog on the shelf. Some hours later, we noticed Belle was missing. Nobody could find Belle. We poked around the house, in the yard, out in the neighborhood, up and down the street calling for her. Finally, Kathryn went in her room to rest and discovered Belle sitting patiently on the bookshelf.

Poor Belle was subjected to acute cognitive dissonance, getting one set of instructions, for instance a tacit "it's OK to pee in the house" from her main caretaker, Kathryn, and a distinctly different set from the rest of us, as in "Belle! Never pee in the house." As a consequence, Belle had a hard time maintaining good manners, particularly in the area of hygiene.

After a year of pet-spotting, I had a dad-fit and went on a carpet rampage. One afternoon, fed up with trying to blot out leaks, I tore through the house and ripped out every carpet and rug in the place. Linda showed more patience than I did, even though some of the carpets were expensive Asian things we'd brought back from travels. Those beyond repair I dumped on the street for the town's annual trash and treasures exercise, a bi-annual event at which Chevy Chase residents would place unwanted or recyclable items on the curb. A parade of people from far and wide would drive by to search for that special something. At the end of the weekend, the city picked up whatever was unwanted. The worst-stained rugs disappeared. The following summer, Kathryn moved to expanded quarters in the basement with tile floors throughout.

The creeping entropy didn't just affect the dog or the house. Magnetic tapes in tape recorders got tangled, Walkmans froze up, jack plugs stopped working. With the onset of more modern devices, passwords evaporated from memory like dew in the hot sun. The kids were savvy enough to make up new ones, but undisciplined enough to not write them down in the flurry of chats or homework. As a result, getting back into computers and phones became a common and maddening chore. Phones had a way of slipping between seats or being left at school (turned off, of course) sitting unfindable in cubbies or desks.

Then there was just plain puzzlement and misunderstanding. One night, while Alana and Linda were away at a school affair, Kathryn came into my room holding something in her hands.

"Dad, how do you do these?"

"Do what, Kathryn? What is that?"

"These butterflies. I don't know how they are supposed to work."

I looked at the Kotex liner she was holding, still not out

of the package, and realized I had entered another lacuna in the curriculum of daddy school.

"Kathryn . . . ," I started out, haltingly. "You know . . . I've never had to try one." Inwardly, my irritation flared at Linda and Alana for not having covered this. But then again, maybe they had. With Kathryn's memory problems, they could have covered it many times and she had simply forgotten.

Kathryn stared at me, blankly. "OK, yeah, but . . . ."

"Let me see." I took the liner and applied my modest engineering skill to decipher the folds and adhesive surfaces. "I guess it goes this way."

"Oh, I see. Right onto the underwear."

"That's right," I said, trying not to disclose too much discovery on my part. "Just sticks right on. Won't move around."

"Gee, thanks, Dad," she said.

"Anytime," I lied.

If things weren't lost, supplies were forgotten. Often, Kathryn would come in at night having discovered that she was down to her last dose of Augmentin medicine. Despite all our best efforts, inventories would run down and be discovered, usually by Kathryn, at the moment stores were ready to close or school was about to start. Our household did not hum like a well-oiled machine with preventive maintenance and anticipatory inventories.

Try as we might, we almost always played catch-up. A sudden dash to replenish, after a typical day when something that was lost needed finding, when something that was forgotten needed remembering, or when half the homework still needed doing—homework we deliberately engaged in to smooth out our anxiety about academic performance.

Repairs were needed at the last minute, when Linda and I were trying to control our anger, when Belle had just peed on the carpet, when pressures from work and the kids piled up past my personal limits. The order of things was never easy to maintain. There simply weren't enough lists, no clever-enough homework systems, not enough alarms to set, not enough bodies to cover the waterfront in a family with asymmetric capabilities.

My work at the World Bank offered a break from the household turbulence, except when I traveled. Even with a live-in au pair, my travel left a big burden on Linda. But there was collateral damage for me as well.

I worked on poverty in cities. This took me to highly stressful places—slums and shantytowns—to work on water and waste issues in cities like Recife, Ho Chi Minh, and Monrovia. Often, I visited sites where kids lived in shacks surrounded by open sewage drainage channels or built on sticks over putrid waters, where nighttime visits to garbage dumps brought me face to face with children the ages of my own scavenging for something to eat, to street corners where a child had a raised arm to shield himself from the next blow by the adult standing there, angry, probably brought to desperation by his own circumstances. I heard the words of an African priest whose life was given over to rescuing children attacked in genocidal war, having limbs cut off by machetes covered by HIV-infected blood.

"Our people are poor," he had said. "They have to mend their lives every day."

These experiences were stressful. But they brought new perspective on caring for my own children. Anger and desperation were emotions I had to subdue constantly at home. The sight of children like my own living in squalor, subjected to inhumane conditions, and condemned to a life of daily mending, gave me fresh gratitude and new energy after I returned.

* * *

One evening, while I was working alone in my office, Eric appeared silently at the door, his eyes red.

"Dad," he began brokenly, his voice barely able to make it through the anguish. "What will become of Kathryn?" My heart sank at seeing his guilt, perhaps buried anger, and the many burdens put on him by his pushed-aside, disabled sister. They hadn't blunted his sense of empathy and caring.

His concern for her suddenly brought out my own. It was a double whammy. My new beat in the hybrid dad model—watching for trouble and engineering compensatory movements—was now punctuated by Eric's heartbreaking insight. He was looking past his own disabilities and beginning to consider her. Perhaps, somewhere lurking behind his question was a dim recognition that he might someday end up being responsible for taking care of her.

I explained that his mother and I had arranged a thing called a trust that would be available for Kathryn as well as for Alana and him. This seemed to relieve him for the time being, but the gnawing source of his concern was never entirely vanquished.

I was going to have to wade into the emotional thicket

Eric was ensnared in and help him understand it, to come to terms with the anxiety and guilt. I put my arm around him, held him, and spoke in low and comforting terms, but I wasn't a natural. I didn't have those "tend and befriend" genes that the Phantom had told me about. I assured him that Kathryn would be all right in the long run, but my own heart ached at the bleak thought of them alone after I was gone.

The Great Flu

The great flu rushed in the door like a bull, raced around the house and left Eric and me moping about like a couple of accident victims in shock.

Wrapped in blankets and feeling lousy, we lit a fire in the living room fireplace to warm our spirits. Smoke filled the room; two smoke alarms went off and wouldn't stop. The fire died and then I finally opened the flue. I burned two neat disks on my fingers closing the fireplace curtain. As Eric was putting Band-Aids on my fingers, Belle decided to poop on the stair landing.

I chased her downstairs. Her mess-making was growing more frequent. She ran with the look of an amateur burglar caught in the act. I was happy to have passed the broom on the way. Belle wasn't so pleased. As I reached the basement landing, I drew a bead on her little butt and threw the broom like a spear, bristle-end first. I hit my target as she reached the last stairstep, and she screamed her fake "he's beating me, he's beating me" yelp and made for the back door.

I chased her outside. This surprised her; she knew this time I meant business. I had never chased her past the threshold. I threw the broom again as she leapt the garden wall. A sharp pain jabbed my shoulder with this throw, a rotator cuff near a tear. I went upstairs through the smoke-filled house and took some Advil. My outburst laid bare the pent-up anger, made less tolerable by the miserable flu. My emotional reserves were spent.

The phone rang. I didn't answer it. I listened for the incoming message. Alana's high school counselor reported that Alana was coming apart. She failed to take a calculator to her calculus test, got a C in a course she was repeating from summer college class, and was falling behind in her computer programming class. Also, she hadn't turned in her photos for the yearbook. The next message was from Eric's psychologist. Many things were going on, she needed to see Linda and me.

That's how the week of June 6, 1996 ended. Little pieces of life kept falling out of order: flu, repairs, dog poop, college applications, grades. A week like most weeks, with the valiant dad leading the anti-entropy team, stepping up to the plate, ducking blame and taking credit for fixing problems; pretending to know all there was to know about busting through lath and plaster and feminine hygiene products, pretending to be a liberal and throwing a broom at my poor little dog, asserting expertise in drawing up lists, concentrating my efforts on mending everything I could find that was mendable, and fending off that which was not.

* * *

We had no shortage of material things that needed mending—hearing aids, toys, tape recorders, Game Boys, bicycles.

My workbench was never clear of gadgets, stray screws, tiny springs. But fatherhood required much more mending than I had ever envisioned. It was much harder to fix the broken promises from friends, broken playdates, the broken hearts brought on by boyfriends and girlfriends who came around and, once they saw the lay of the land, silently moved on.

Before illness and disability was a family of three marked by easy routine. Emotionally and logistically, we looked forward to knowing what to expect and how to recover if some small perturbation cropped up—a carpool shift, for instance, or a playdate adjustment. With illness and disability, the world changed deep within me and outside, around me.

On top of that, Linda and I had psycho-emotional compasses pointed in diametrically opposite directions.

One morning, I put my coffee in the microwave and pushed the button. Ants scurried around the counter. I looked down at the increasing depth of wrinkle in the skin gathered above my knee. Then the ants again. I began to identify with their workaholic lives, but resented their utter lack of wrinkles, the absence of slack anywhere.

Linda entered the kitchen, ignoring Alana. Her forward bearing projected a sense of mission. Ants walk in the same posture always; humans lean into the wind when they have something to accomplish.

"You're letting Kathryn off way too easily," Linda declared. "She needs to stay on her budget."

I turned to her, fed up with the third round on the same topic. Kathryn was spending too much money on chai lattes at Starbucks. This small battle was like all large wars about some-

thing more symbolic—a view of autonomy, a sense of threatened dignity, a power struggle protracted over many decades, a
war long over—but a battle still being fought.

"Linda, you can't teach lessons by beating her with a stick,"
I blasted back.

"Shut the fuck up!" A trumpet blast louder than the first
came from Alana, standing off to the side. In a single stroke,
she maneuvered to become the adult in the room. She was
talking to me. I glared in stunned silence.

My daughter was assuming a posture much like my own
father's. She struck a contradictory pose—her arms akimbo,
small fire in her eyes, her face twisted, fed up with her parents
bickering. Not an ounce of sympathy was anywhere on her
face. A drill instructor had jumped out spontaneously. She was
showing the same resolve about our dustups as she showed
about mentoring Kathryn.

But where was I in all this? Where was the three-year-old
I remember running to pull my bags off the baggage conveyor
after returning home from a long journey? Where was the kid
who offered me magic rivets?

That was the moment when everything changed. There was
a pivot from my being chief rulemaker to being co-rulemaker.
And it didn't come when Alana had answered my appeal a couple of years earlier to help with the kids. It came at a moment
when she was calling for me to behave. It was at a time of
exasperation for Linda and me in our marriage. My behavior
triggered Alana's ascendance to co-rulemaker. And I deserved
the demotion.

Alana had grown fed up with her parents' quarrels, perhaps

because she was in the process of growing closer to her future partner and beginning to see a new way of doing things. And the same was true for me. I could see that the time had come for me to step down. After all, I had begged her for a long time to get into the family game. At that pivotal moment, she accepted it and moved ahead. Just not in the way I had hoped. Though it caused painful friction between us, as the children advanced through school, they gradually acquired the discipline that Linda imparted, as well as the staying-focused-on-the-big-picture that I offered. As a team, we had a complete package, but our personal touch had different weights and our rhythms were out of sync. Over time, we rediscovered and mutually acknowledged our respective roles and deepened our appreciation for the contributions we each made.

Mending the tears in our marriage was not easy. One of my closest friends knew about the details of our family and the pressures we felt. Many times, he offered solace and compassion.

"Yes, it's hard," I confided to him. "But I will never leave her." My words came out effortlessly and without premeditation. The tensions were great, yes, but the bond was still exceedingly strong. I knew that from the very moment Linda and I had made our vow at Kathryn's bedside when she was near death. That vow meant staying together, keeping our parenting intact. That would need mending, too, from time to time.

I worried that I was going to make mistakes, and of course, I did. It's inevitable, so I had to be ready to mend. And when I worried that I wasn't up to the mending, caution crept in and defined a new point on the arc of fatherhood. Fixing things and relationships took me away from exploring with the kids, from going to the edge. If I didn't go myself, or let my kids take some risks, I would end up being overcautious like my dad, and my kids would end up being like him, too, not able to venture out and feel the ripples of success from a risk well run.

PART V

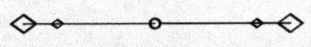

LIFTOFF

TENNIS, A BOX OF RAIN, AND STARDUST

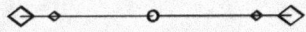

"**I** am hitting hard," Alana replied, a little peeved at her high school tennis coach. Alana paused, laying down her racket. She looked down and raised her hand to signal she needed a moment from the intensity of her lesson. She had been striking the ball carefully, with good technique, but so controlled that her game was underpowered. The coach saw that her fire was boxed up inside. He pressed her in a friendly but demanding way.

"I want to see much greater pace on the ball," he insisted.

Alana turned to face the ball feeder again. She was beginning her second year of high school, and the tennis coach saw promise in her athleticism and smooth strokes.

"OK," Alana muttered, her words barely making it to the surface. She glanced up to me, sitting nearby in the spectator stands. She acquiesced because the coach wanted it, not because I wanted or indeed, that she did. She uncoiled on the next feed and sent the ball rocketing back. Ten more balls she slammed. *Whop, whop, whop,* each stroke perfectly timed, smooth, and flowing, each ball snapped back with a sharp report as her racket slammed into it. Her motion was the same smooth motion, but she was starting from a deeper unwinding, her back swing drawn much further around. Beads of sweat popped out on her brow, and wet regions were spreading on her jersey. Her soft audible exertions became loud emphatic grunts. At the end of the session, she sat staring at the court.

"Alana!" I exclaimed, coming down from my seat. I turned to her squarely, an expression of surprise and discovery on my face. "I've never seen you hit the ball like that."

"Me neither," she panted. She flashed a little sheepish smile, a hint of reluctance kept it from breaking out more broadly, as though she didn't recognize or didn't want to own the power that she had just demonstrated.

"It started with the frozen yogurt, remember, Dad?" She was referring to learning tennis when she was eight years old. Back then in Berkeley, I promised her frozen yogurt if she could hit ten in a row back to me. Now she was on the threshold of becoming a woman. Something new had been drawn out of hiding this day on the court. She possessed a power she was not sure she wanted and often hid.

I thought of my Phantom. The one who protected me from fatherly retributions by stopping me short of reaching personal bests in sports. Was fear of retribution from me, or perhaps some guilt about succeeding when her siblings were struggling, sapping her will to perform? Did they keep Alana from reaching new heights? If that were true, I could perhaps do something for her that my father wasn't able to do for me. Perhaps I could calm her Phantom, but I didn't know where to start.

The turbulence put in Alana's path by her siblings and parents gave her plenty of twists and turns to deal with. Linda had arranged for Alana to have consultation with the wonderful psychiatrist, EJA, whom Alana saw intermittently over a five-year period during high school and college. He was vital in helping her stay ahead of the waves of emotional bumpiness she was experiencing.

EJA was especially good at getting Alana to see the glass half full, of changing her perspective, converting the family nightmare of difficulties into a story about survival. He made an important contribution by getting her to see things not as disaster but as reality that could be managed. Above all, his psychiatric expertise helped Alana to keep in touch, even as she broke away from us. She was able to find a pathway to independence while maintaining an availability and graciousness toward the rest of the family.

Of course, I wanted to be the author of those insights and guidance for Alana. I wanted to be the holder of the soft light to show the path forward. That image was the natural extension of my idyllic model of fatherhood that now seemed impossibly lost in the past. But I realized that being that kind of father had been buried long ago under mounting requirements of her siblings and the bickering between Linda and me.

Instead, my best course was to be a quiet supporter of EJA, to encourage Alana to see him whenever she felt it necessary. He was an adjunct, another resource that Linda had found. And now, in a sense, I was becoming an adjunct as well. Though my relationship with Alana remained strong, I worried that I wouldn't be able to recapture that special magic we'd shared for so long. I was pleasantly surprised when, one night during her senior year in high school, Alana washed away my worries.

We were enjoying a quiet moment alone together in her room.

"Listen to this, Dad," she said. "I think you'll like it." She handed me headphones. "It's from your time."

I looked at her with wonder and slipped the headphones over my ears. A tune began.

What do you want me to do,
to do for you to see you through?
For this is all a dream we dreamed
one afternoon long ago.

I recognized it as the Grateful Dead, but I couldn't name the tune. "What is it, Alana?" I mouthed, headphones still in place.

"The Dead," she said. "Box of Rain."

I nodded, straining to keep the grimace on my face from revealing an emotional outbreak. A small dam inside was giving way. She had picked something from my past, yet it was hers, something she found on her own, not a tune I suggested or showed her. The previous year she had wanted to attend a Dead concert. I had said no. My conservative impulses had won out. She was upset, but because she was only seventeen, I held out. The next year, Jerry Garcia died. I felt badly for Alana, an opportunity to see an icon from my time that she wanted and couldn't have.

The lyrics of the tune she showed me described my

growing reliance upon her for help, and her growing need to find her own path in life—a pathway out of the turmoil of the family. And now she was sharing this with me.

Walk out of any doorway
feel your way, feel your way
like the day before
Maybe you'll find direction
around some corner
where it's been waiting to meet you.

Each passage was loaded with meaning for us. Alana was now well into adolescence, but I already saw her as a young adult, glimpsing the brightness of womanhood, putting a family nightmare behind her. In subtle ways, she revealed a mature presence in her judgments, the suggestions she made about handling her siblings, the choices she made with friends. Showing me this tune was in itself a gesture of solidarity.

I looked up at Alana. She wore a sly, knowing smile. Tears were in both our eyes. The quiet, unspoken bond was thick around us, up to our hips in emotional molasses of common understanding.

We embraced. Father and daughter, person to person, one collaterally wounded to another. An old veteran of internecine battles hugging a young recruit. The rhythmical tunes of the Dead washed around us. My mind raced back quickly to a magical moment when she was four years old and had awakened before sunrise to say goodbye as I was preparing for a long consulting mission in Africa.

A decade later that bond was stronger than ever. Alana

was giving me a gift, a sentiment from my own past, a metaphorical box of rain, our storm made tiny enough for us to handle.

A box of rain will ease the pain and love will see you through.

The following summer, we sat under a starlit sky on Hilton Head Island. Meteorites streaked across our view like supersonic fireflies tracing dazzling straight lines.

"I saw Halley's Comet a couple of years back, from Teresa's house in Petropolis," I recalled. Our closest friends had a summer place in the hills outside Rio. "The comet was easily visible with the naked eye. It stood there motionless up next to the stars."

"Cool, Daddy. I would love to see that." She thought for a moment. "These guys are rocks," she said confidently, gesturing to the sky. "They come from further out in the solar system."

"Ooohh, so glad to see that science class is paying off." A greater payoff than I had ever imagined.

Alana beamed. "Yeah, and all that fiery tail is just a little more dust to float out there in space." She turned to me. "Like us, right, Daddy?"

"Yes, sweetie, pretty much like us, down here all formed and organized—dust put together into super-complicated life-forms eventually to get back up there."

"Stardust," she said. "We're stardust."

TILT-A-WHIRL AND ROCKETS

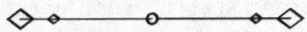

One night later that year, Eric and I sat together watching an animated sitcom about a child in Texas who had ADHD. In the TV episode, the child had taken a medication similar to the one prescribed for Eric. The child on TV was playing checkers. In the middle of the game, he began to stare intently at an ordinary checkers piece. He looked up at his dad and said pensively, "Gee, Dad, this piece has 387 edges and that piece only has 386."

I looked at Eric. "Gee, E, is that what it's like?"

"Exactly, Dad," he said, looking at me, stone-faced.

Fathering Eric was a rolling discovery. The stunning finding of his hearing loss was only the beginning. A decade later, Linda found a renowned specialist in the brain development of teens, who was conducting research at the National Institutes of Health (NIH). He explained that because Eric's hearing loss began at an early age, it had cascading effects. When the young, developing brain doesn't get the full complement of stimuli it expects—auditory, visual, tactile—brain development is thrown askew. For instance, circuits involved in hearing get mixed up with those involved in vision. That in turn comes with effects on attention, comprehension, and self-control.

One outcome for Eric was auditory processing difficulties. Eric can't hear in the same way other kids do because of a disconnect between the ears and the brain. The brain can't so easily recognize and interpret speech. Another problem was that Eric exhibited symptoms of ADHD (attention deficit and hyperactivity disorder).

ADHD is a collection of symptoms, including trouble focusing attention, concentrating on tasks, and listening well to directions. Eric wasn't hyperactive or impulsive, like some ADHD children are. On the contrary. He was dreamy, easygoing and compliant. But he did have difficulty zeroing in on tasks and keeping his attention focused.

These symptoms spilled over into executive function problems for Eric, like the inability to work in an organized, coordinated way in setting goals, making plans and keeping track of time, focusing on tasks and details. Several kinds of medication can increase powers of concentration. That's what the checkers story illustrated.

Testing at NIH and by private evaluators also showed that Eric had a very high IQ, much like Alana's, but the disabilities sapped his intellectual power. The expert at NIH provided the first comprehensive diagnosis of Eric's condition along with a medication that worked for him.

Eric had to exert a great deal of energy in life just to keep up. Emotional stress and psychological issues accumulated. Troubled by devices—both hearing aids as well as other sound-amplification equipment in the classroom—he felt the sting of ostracism, not always in an active way, but also passively, as in invitations that weren't extended, friendships that didn't get a start.

In elementary school he experienced biting put-downs. One day at a fourth-grade summer camp, a little girl had cut in line in front of Eric.

"What's up?" he asked, his large hearing aids clearly within view. She replied without hesitation, "I'm perfect, you're not."

At other times, the discrimination was subtler, like not getting invited for sleepovers, play groups, or outings.

I was unprepared then for what Eric really needed. I found myself having to run to catch up, for instance in the baseball coaching days. The other fathers tolerated my excesses, but I didn't see the misguidedness in it until years later. What he really needed was my just being there, to watch, have fun, and take him to college or pro games to stimulate and inspire him.

While the line cut-ins and ostracism were hurtful, perhaps the most punishing thing for Eric, and the most difficult fatherhood problem, was having to cope with Kathryn's neediness, which often cut into Eric's space. Still struggling with her own disabilities, she used Eric as a crutch—mental, emotional, and sometimes physical. A slow accumulation of frustration finally boiled over one day when he blurted out to her: "Stop using my brain!"

No matter how hard we tried, it was not possible to soothe away the antagonisms engendered by their disabilities.

As the kids grew older, I engineered more one-on-one times, trying to compensate for the long weeks I was away, to dedicate time and focus on each of them individually. Deep inside, I felt that Eric needed the most attention. In the great scheme of life, he was born into the shadow of Kathryn's disability, whereas at least Alana had had undivided attention for more than three years. I recognized that this kind of calculation was imprecise and maybe not really an accurate way to gauge need, but it was all I had.

I was worried about being able to make good on my hybrid model of fatherhood. I put myself on the lookout for signs of the Phantom, my own excessive caution with Eric, and planned to try harder to explore emotional terrain with him. When Eric was ten, we went on a couple of memorable father-son outings away from the home for a week or so.

Tilt-A-Whirl

The boardwalk at Ocean City in Maryland was one big fluff of cotton candy sprinkled with teenage girls parading in denim cutoffs. They were moving experiments in lipstick and rouge, with bouffant hair curled high above their brows. They giggled along in clutches of five and six. At age eleven, Eric was drawn as much to the intrusive, siren sounds of the video arcade as to the little bottoms waddling along the boardwalk. We fell in with the crowd, strolling the scene. We stopped twice for ice cream. I let him play video games.

Then we pulled out our mitts and played catch. In the afternoon, we dropped into the CVS and bought a pair of scissors. I cut his hair while we sat on the beach. We went to the amusement park.

Eric tried for an hour, pitching quarters at the bottles to win a panda bear.

"Try again, E," I said. "You'll get it." I was ready to indulge him.

Eric looked up, his face still a little chubby, his expression tight and exasperated. Small beads of sweat formed on his forehead. He took some more dollars and resumed pitching. His quarters bounced aimlessly away. I could see a familiar smarting behind the sweating. Eric's mouth turned down; his lip tightened. Eric wasn't uncoordinated. This pitching task required not just concentration, but patience and lots of luck.

After many more quarters, the booth attendant, a guy in his fifties, lifted his long stick, snagged a large bear hanging from the netting overhead, and extended the bear to Eric. He cast a knowing look at me. "Here, guy," he said quietly to Eric, "you've earned it." He wore a sympathetic resignation on his face. Eric fought back tears, trying mightily to preserve his dignity, to be a man.

"Thank you," Eric said, quietly, looking down as he took the bear.

I didn't do as well. I couldn't find the right words to balance appreciation with consolation. Tears were threatening a jailbreak. I could only wave a salute to the attendant. His eyes and a subtle nod gave me all the cover I needed.

* * *

We went shopping, poking into small stores for water toys and boats and inflatable life rafts and softballs and other paraphernalia. We found a drugstore for hearing aid batteries.

"Let me try your hearing aids," I said. I wanted to see what Eric experienced every day. They didn't fit that well, but they stayed in. I put the setting on normal. The experience opened a different world.

Someone entered through the aluminum frame door in the small shop. It had made an unpleasant, small screech I barely noticed when we walked in. With Eric's hearing aids it sounded like a howler monkey. Scuffling shoes and rustling papers came through like a mounting thunderstorm. Speech was magnified out of proportion. It was shocking.

"Eric, how do you put up with all this noise?"

He gave me a sidewise grin. "You get used to it, Daddy."

My heart sank. My kids had been wearing these devices for years, and I hadn't appreciated how off-putting they were, how disruptive they could be. My view of Eric's world grew drearier. At that moment, my optimism fell a few degrees. I realized anew that the stairclimb for Eric to reach a plane of equality was much steeper than I realized. Much more needed to be done. Yet, I already felt I was moving at full capacity.

* * *

We went back to the amusement park. A loud clatter rose above the chaotic pitch of the carnival atmosphere. A woman started her ride around a circular track, the only passenger on the Tilt-A-Whirl. The train of giant teacup carts picked up pace. She raced along the track in her personal cup, a train horn blasting as she gained speed on the circuit.

BLARRRRRRE, went the horn, loud and penetrating, like the warning blast of a speeding freight train sounding out into the evening sky. The cups were spinning wildly as they hurtled along. The track lifted on one side as she raced and whirled amid the rumble and blare of the horn. She was riding a life like my own, a controlled catastrophe in a teacup. Not another person on the entire train, racing around wildly, caught in a circle at high speed, not going off the track but not getting anywhere at all. Round and round, leaving and arriving at the same spot.

Her hands slipped around her thighs, searching down into the pocket between her legs. The woman seeking pleasure—hidden only by the chaos of the speeding contraption, the racket of the cups on the track, and the blaring horn—struck me as a parody of myself. Where was pleasure? She openly accepted, even made use, of her circumstances as camouflage for finding solace. I constantly denied mine. I stared in silence, Eric at my side. His eyes were elsewhere. *BLARRRRRE* again, the Tilt-A-Whirl gained a powerful momentum, the sound earning the pitch of the locomotive horn. Her head was thrown back, her eyes closed, her hands pressed tight, around and around, the horn sounding louder, more intrusive, like a train was coming right at that moment. Like me, she was seeking some comfort, going in circles. I held Eric's shoulder. *Get out of the way! Clear the tracks! We're going nowhere!*

* * *

We took a roller-coaster ride. I had promised Eric, despite my fears of being too old for roller coasters and memories of a bad back being jolted on herky-jerky trains riding over steel rails bolted onto soaring wooden structures. But this train glided over welded steel tubes, a welcome, computer-assisted design: smooth, continuous, no clickety-clack. The ride was more like flying a small jet plane than riding a jerky steam locomotive.

Looking ahead, I saw the tracks bend into a curve and realized as we swerved left, that yes, I'm going around in a steep bank.

"We're turning on our side," I called out, loudly—uselessly—to Eric. The spin and roll incident flashed in my mind. My butt pressed into the seat, right arm squished to the side. Eric's body pressed into mine. Then, as we pulled out, I could see the track ahead rear up in front of us, and I knew it was going to be a loop.

We climbed and reached an apogee; we bent over slowly rolling backward and began to pick up speed. I looked up to the ground. "We're going over the top, E," I yelled out again. "Here we goooo!" Useless as my commentary was for Eric, the narrative was helping me get through my fears. We plunged downward. Eric was quiet, his eyes wide, mouth reflected a gleeful fall, newly cropped hair blown back in the wind. "AAAAHHHHH," we shrieked exuberantly.

Rockets

In February 1996, in an effort for Eric and me to get away from the turmoil of home, I arranged for tickets to view the launch of a NASA shuttle. We landed in Orlando, Florida, on a beautiful clear day, a promising omen for our father-son adventure a thousand miles away from unrelenting demands of disability back home.

We plunged into an exciting adventure. I rented a white Mustang convertible and drove east to Cape Canaveral to view the launch of NASA's STS 75. We put down the car top and turned our baseball caps backward. The radio blasted out rock music.

At the Cape, we visited the outdoor museum of rockets and gaped at the monstrous tractor used to move the rocket to the launch pad. The next morning, we anxiously searched to find our places at NASA's viewing spot for the launch.

Our crowd of a couple of hundred "VIPs" were gathered on a small viewing hill a few miles from the launch pad. My only entrée to VIP status was the good luck of living across the street from a neighbor related to the NASA administrator.

The countdown was nearing. I was tense, almost jittery. I fumbled to focus my binoculars on the magnificent white rocket sitting on the launch pad on the horizon. Eric was by my side, striking a parallel pose. I was like a kid, always interested in rockets and airplanes. Eric and I had made model airplanes, Star Wars speeders, and rubber band wind-ups. We had spent afternoons setting off small model rockets at a park in Chevy Chase. We cherished those scenes, miniatures of the real thing at the Cape. *Columbia* was to carry a novel tethering line to generate electricity for the space station. The placid day contrasted with our nervous energy.

As liftoff drew nearer, every face was alive with wide eyes, every movement jerky or clipped. With our fellow observers, we quickly reached a moment impossible to rehearse. There was no preparing for the inchoate buzz of anticipation. Anxious that we might miss something, we second-guessed our every gesture, every movement, fidgeting, never confident that we had the right settings on our cameras, the right viewing angle. *Glasses on or off? Hat. Where's my hat?* Wanting time to slow, to take stock, I mentally reviewed my every movement. We anticipated a grand technological feat, something powerful, historic, otherworldly. My pulse quickened; my mouth was dry.

"Eric. Be sure and stay close by me," I said nervously. "It's easy to get lost here." Our viewing area was closed and guarded, but still, bad things can happen. I knew from experience. Kathryn had been hit by a one-in-a-million virus. "Don't go beyond those ropes," I cautioned. NASA had cordoned off the perimeter with bright yellow rope. "It's for safety."

"OK, Dad," Eric said patiently.

He surveyed our surroundings. We were gathered atop a sand dune, a spot organized by NASA with loudspeakers, latrines, and water. Our safety zone was created after the *Challenger* disaster a decade before, but we were as close to the launch pad as anyone outside of NASA could get. Off in the distance, the shuttle was white and gleaming, hugging its boosters and giant orange fuel pods.

The energy in our small part of the world crackled like the frequent updates that came over the loudspeakers.

"T-minus ninety seconds and counting," came the resonant voice of mission control over the PA.

Eric looked up with a lifetime of eagerness gathered in one giddy moment and asked. "Is it going to go now?"

"Yes, Eric. We are close. They are going to begin the countdown . . . if nothing goes wrong."

"Coming up on go for an auto-sequence start," came the

voice. A shower of sparks spit at the rocket nozzles, and tiny bursts of smoke emerged at the base of the launch pad.

Our briefing books provided a timeline and narrative of the launch. The sequence was methodical and precise, a long series of steps with liner notes down to minutes and seconds. The pages were filled with coordinating instructions and periodic bailout points in case a mishap threatened the mission.

All this contrasted so sharply with my carefree attitude toward life and fate. Before fatherhood, my view of life was an unchoreographed, carefree movement. I was Zorba, dancing on the beach with one hand waving free. I couldn't be troubled; I didn't want to be burdened by the caution that was behind all this meticulous planning and careful scripting that characterized NASA. Yet my devil-may-care approach to life had been blasted away by the virus. The careful preparations in this launch were a lesson in daddy school. Script some of it; you can't leave it all to fate.

My pulse quickened. A hushed silence fell over the crowd. "... five, four, three ..."

I glanced down, eager to share with Eric. My heart jumped. He had disappeared. *Fuck!!* I swept the crowd quickly. The spectators were a slapdash of shapes and sizes, jumbles of bright pri-mary colors pocked with heads and hats and dark glasses. He was half the size of most adults and not in view.

"... seven, six, we have a go for main engine start ..."

"... two, one, booster ignition and liftoff—liftoff for the shuttle *Columbia* ..."

A frantic surge swept over me. Things can go wrong, even here. I twisted inside but could not resist turning back to the launch pad. I pushed back against my fears.

A typhoon of white clouds erupted from beneath *Columbia*, enveloping it like a gigantic cloak. From our vantage point, the air was eerily still. The rocket moved in silence. It rose slowly and crept upward. The crowd fell in a hush, mesmerized like me. I stole a glance at my side to check for Eric again. He was still out of sight. The air remained silent. Torn again, I flitted over the thought to race after him and then paused. Just another moment to witness the climax. He couldn't be far. The area was closed. It would only be a moment.

A thundering vibration hit my ears and penetrated to the pit of my stomach. The deafening blast paralyzed me. The sound shook every fiber of my being. A wave of goosebumps traveled down my midsection, passed across my scrotum, and reached my ankles. Eric had disappeared, and I was in an emotional blender, equal parts exhilaration and anxiety, shaking emotionally and physically. The roar whipped it all together, shattering thoughts, blanketing my panic about Eric. I was frozen in time but riveted to the four-and-a-half-million-pound machine now rising into the sky.

An incandescent tongue of flame shot downward. A bright white column followed *Columbia* upward. Far below the tail, the brilliant white faded to pale yellow before darkening to a gray.

Another crackle in the PA system. "Houston, roll program!" said the pilot. "Roger roll, *Columbia*," came the response from Houston.

The ensemble of shuttle, thrusters, and external fuel tank arched high into the sky and began a slow roll. The trail grew longer, tracing the climb. At the head of the column sat the shrinking speck of the rocket, its shattering, catastrophic thunder beginning to fade.

I stared in admiration at the feat that had been accomplished. The rocket, so cleanly engineered, so utterly opposite from that rocket-virus in our lives. Ours couldn't be scripted like this *Columbia*. It could only be mastered after the fact. To master that great ugly fate that came streaking into our lives required a different kind of engineering.

I thought, Yeah, we suffered, we suffered a lot, but we've come out of it, and we are still standing. Fuck you, Fate.

Cheers and yelling, clapping and shouting, meekly broke through the receding roar. I couldn't keep my eyes off the shuttle and couldn't keep my mind off Eric.

Then, underneath my gaze, there he was: Eric stood right in front of me, staring up at me again, a smile on his face as wide as the moon.

"Wasn't that great, Dad?"

"Eric! Where were you? You scared me to death."

"I just went down out in front of the ropes. It's the only place I could see."

Right there, I saw Eric inching upward, riding a small launch forward. I stared back at him, beholding something new, something refreshing and welcome. The rocket was gone. And while it was leaving, Eric had taken his place in the world where he could see, a small step forward to view the sky. He broke some rules.

"Yes, Eric. It was absolutely terrific."

Though short and too few, the outings with Eric served

their purpose. They helped us reset our connection and helped me gain a deeper understanding of his challenges. And like that "we're still standing" moment at the blast off, our trips offered the occasional breakthrough—of having come through a crisis, of having reached a turning point, of having tamed the Phantom and of celebrating small bends in the arc of fatherhood.

ALANA HOLDS UP HER SKY

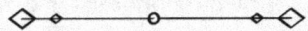

Even before Alana had finished high school, she quietly undertook a new role in the family. She became a more mature caretaker, an opinion giver, a consultant. She came to have more say in our lives. And that transition into her adulthood proved to be a bumpy one for all of us.

Several years earlier, when Kathryn was still in high school, without warning she began to show signs of tachycardia, a run of chaotic and unproductive heartbeats. One afternoon, a babysitter found her passed out on our couch. If her cardio self-regulation system hadn't self-corrected, she could have had seizures, or even died. I feared that this was the danger period we had been warned about in the very beginning. Patients like Kathryn who survive myocarditis at an early age don't come out unscathed. Scar tissue formed during the infection can interrupt electrical timing of heartbeats and this can be a problem, even fatal, when they become teenagers. When they enter rapid growth spurts, kids with a history of myocarditis can go into heart failure due to the sudden increase in the pumping load. That fear loomed up and haunted us.

On top of that, Kathryn and Eric had entered a period of more difficult schoolwork. Linda hadn't eased up on her standards, and I continued looking for a calmer, less stressful pathway through the nightly academic chores. I had begun to run aground with Linda in managing the kids. At the same time, pressures at work were piling up as I made my way through a new and unfamiliar part of the bureaucracy at the World Bank.

Linda and I were edging into desperation. More than a decade of dealing with disabilities, and now this new danger of sudden heart failure for Kathryn. Whether she realized it or not, Alana, gifted and mature, was breaking into proto-parenting.

Alana was already an adult in my eyes, but veering away at the same time, trying to live her life as a teenager, to escape from the insatiable emotional imperatives of caring for her siblings and being caught in the crossfire of bickering parents. She sat with her legs crossed, studying her parents with a sympathetic eye. She wore khakis and a white blouse. With minimum makeup and hair up in back, she looked older than her years.

With the news of Kathryn's new vulnerability, I sat with Linda and Alana in our bedroom as we made ready to retire for the night. I felt we were staring over a new cliff. The little ones were already asleep. I began to vent anxiety I didn't know how to handle.

"We've done all we can," I announced in vague exasperation, speaking out into the room as if my pleading would somehow recruit help from Alana, at that time, eighteen.

Her eyes swayed between her parents and the doorway. She rose and began to pace, seeing where I was headed and wanting not to be trapped at home. It ran against her urge to salvage her teenage life. We needed help with Kathryn, with the kids' homework, medicines, discipline. Alana needed to be living a normal teenager's life.

I ran through a dialogue in my own mind, saying to her, We never wanted your life to be like this. We wanted to be able to give you so much more. We are so depressed we cannot give it to you. Now we want you to give it to us.

"Alana," I paused. She stared at me. "We need your help," I continued. It was a plea, a prayer, a preposterous out-loud hope of bringing her in, to substitute for Linda and me.

"I am already helping with their homework, with driving, with everything," she countered. She was right, but it was more than help I needed. I sensed she knew that. It was salvation I needed. I was looking for a way out.

"You have to suck it up, Alana," I declared, accusingly. That could have been my father accusing me of selfishness after the death of my schoolmate forty-five years earlier. My high school classmate was my template for teenage life. He had lasted three months after diagnosis of a lymphoma and died at age seventeen. After his death, I plunged into a tailspin, the role model for my life ripped away. My father told me to suck it up then.

"I've already sucked it up," she shot back, her face beginning to distort, her voice quivering, tears seeping out of her eyes. "I've done more than my share."

She nailed me. She was spot on, and I knew it immediately. I was shocked at my own breach, taken aback by my naked desperation. Several years earlier, she had already drawn a line about her

parent's bickering. Now she was clarifying the line between her parents and parenting. That was not her task. Besides, I wasgrasping for help from my daughter who had already given so much. Her response was the sort I should have given my dad.

* * *

A few months later, I found Alana deep in thought, her face long, head in hand, her shoulders hunched over her keyboard.

"Writing my college essay," she said, softly, as I entered the room. "It's about the rainbow wires," she said.

"Rainbow?"

"When Kathryn came home from the doctors with a sprout of wires—all different colors coming from under her blouse." I nodded in recognition. The previous week, Kathryn had returned from the latest of many appointments at Children's Hospital Medical Center in Washington wearing a portable heart monitor. The cardiologists were probing for the extent of Kathryn's abnormality. They had never seen a near-adult patient like Kathryn who had recovered from a viral myocarditis. Color-coded electrical contact ribbons protruded from beneath her blouse. The cardiac unit was hoping to record the frequency and severity of her abnormal heartbeats.

Alana continued. "There was dumb shock on her face, a bit of bewilderment in her eyes when she came in the door and saw me . . . and tears in my eyes when I caught sight of her," Alana managed. That was the week that Kathryn had slipped into unconsciousness in our living room. She had had a flurry of fibrillations. The sight of the familiar rainbow wires rang up interior alarms in all of us.

I put my arm around Alana. We sat quietly for a few moments. "I'm OK," she said. "A little shaky at first." She held onto my hand. "The wires were like a prompt." She looked away at her screen. "I'm going to write my essay about it." She was preparing her applications for university. "It wasn't just the shock of heart stuff, again," she said. "It brought back memories of the green line."

Alana was referring to an episode when Kathryn, still an infant, was first hospitalized following a mysterious disease. I had been called urgently to the hospital where Kathryn was being examined. The doctors were puncturing Kathryn's eardrum, checking to determine if an inner ear infection was behind her undiagnosed malady. With no childcare for Alana, then three, I had brought her with me to the hospital.

Because of infection controls, Alana wasn't allowed to accompany me into Kathryn's room. In desperation, I had placed her on a chair at the green line, marking the point—only yards from Kathryn's alcove—beyond which child visitors were not allowed to go.

I mustered all my most caring, fatherly words, letting her know she would not be out of my sight. From her spot with a few books and a child's board game, I walked backward down the hallway keeping eye contact with Alana.

"You have a special place at the line," I promised. "Daddy only has to peek in this room, right here, to talk with the doctors." Alana was not fooled. She stared at me with a brave face. "Don't worry, sweetie, I'm not going any further than here." I stopped in my tracks, as if to punctuate my sincerity. Then, continuing my slow pace backward, I continued. "See? Here I am. Now don't you move," I said, drawing out the 'ooove.' I turned my head away from Alana briefly to speak through the doorway with the doctor and Linda, doing my best to not lose sight of Alana. She turned to her toys and games, busying herself in her little play station at the line.

But the damage was done. She was already being abandoned. I was in the act of desertion. She knew it and so did I. A little piece of the sky fell right there. Right inside the hospital.

My sky-holding impulse had begun even before that green line trauma; it had begun the night Kathryn survived, my father died, and I had to tell Alana about our loss. From that moment on, I had seen myself as the defiant face grimacing at the overpowering blast of fate that was obliterating my life as I had imagined it. I was vigilant, always looking for ways to keep the damage from spilling over onto her world. I thought I might have succeeded a little in that task. But I was now realizing that though I thought that something was achieved, sky-holding was no longer the most important role for me, after all.

Alana's preparation for her undergraduate work was now peeling back the cover on a small window through which I could see where the sky had landed. The essays—the ones

required for application to university—traversed much of
her early childhood. It reached into regions I hadn't realized
were a part of her development. I began to see more clearly
than ever the long-term effects on her from the speeding,
out-of-control freight train that carried her little sister. I was
confronted for the first time in decades with collateral damage. They were large chunks of the fallen sky lying around for
everyone to see.

The chunks took the form of clouds of doubt that damp-
ened Alana's spirit and turned her away from trying something new; they were the impulses to help others first, even
to her own detriment; they were shadows of guilt about her
siblings' misfortunes. The fallen sky became dampers inside
her soul that squeezed off the more daring ideas about life,
and the tiny pincers that crimped down her handwriting to
neatly formed letters so compact that they seemed to want
to be hidden from view, to find obscurity on the page so that
no one could read them, lest they detect the vestiges of fear,
danger, and anger, all lurking inside.

At the very least anyway, these were my fears. If Alana really did share them, she mostly succeeded in concealing them.
I feared that the smooth gracefulness with which she conduct-
ed her life camouflaged anxiety and intense deliberation. And
for much of her life, try as I might, I didn't make much of a
dent. Yes, we were close, yes, we still had a vibrant, inner bond
that shimmered with "Box of Rain" moments. But I feared
that all that was not enough to see her through, not enough to
smooth out the rutted, internal pathway she was traveling.

It wasn't easy for a gifted kid like Alana, for anybody in their teens, struggling to find her own identity, to have siblings so visibly different from her friends and her peers. Not easy to negotiate awkward introductions on the odd occasion when friends stayed overnight or came by for parties. Alana was independent and reliable. In middle and high school, she took AP courses, made excellent grades, and required very little help with homework. For many years, she was like a child adult from nineteenth-century England, an adult by the time she was ten. Starting in the sixth grade, she would rise at six-thirty a.m., walk herself to the bus stop from our apartment in DC, and get herself home after school. She was kind of a latchkey kid, except that her parents were home, preoccupied with her brother and sister.

* * *

Kathryn and Eric each had a special group of friends. Kathryn's group I called the Children of Paradise. One member of the group had a dozen operations on his spinal cord before he was fifteen. Clumsy mechanical leg braces ran from his shin to his thigh. He walked with a lurching gate. I often worried that a small dip in sidewalk elevation would cause a fall. Another girl had severe dyslexia. She was at sea trying to read and embarrassed in class. But she possessed an innate morality strong enough to invite the awkward lurching boy into their group. The fourth member of the Children of Paradise was a boy who had brain anoxia from birth with consequences more serious and visible than Kathryn's. Their individual disabilities were the glue that held them together.

They were outcasts, but sweet and caring with one another.

Eric's friends were teammates from soccer, baseball, and video games. The video game group—they were called the Fearsome Five—was a small United Nations. An Argentine, an Indian, a couple of Americans—one Black, the other a classic nerdy geek—plus Eric with his hearing aids and slurred, nasally speech. Each had a particular attribute that disqualified them from the in-groups at school. Altogether, the Children of Paradise and the Fearsome Five were unusual and eye-catching, sometimes disruptive, often odd and socially awkward, and above all, more intrusive and less cool than the younger siblings of Alana's peers.

And yet, Alana was protective. She had strong sibling loyalty. She would coach Kathryn in soccer, answer questions and help with math, do Kathryn's barrettes and braids, and help them remember their medicines. One night on vacation, she and Kathryn snuck out of our condo while everyone else was asleep and had a swim in the pool across the street. They howled with surprise and laughter when they came face to face with a frog taking his own midnight swim.

At other times, Alana would hack into Kathryn's online chats to pick up questionable exchanges concerning hot topics, like boys, sex, menstruation, and relationships with friends. When she found issues, she would pick her time to bring up the topic with her sister and turn it into a learning moment to help Kathryn steer through the thistles and confusion of life as a teenager.

* * *

Alana told me about the night she walked into the TV room, surprising Kathryn, who was alone with a boy. Her story went like this.

"Hi, Kathryn," she said. A moment of silence fell. The boy fidgeted. Kathryn looked away. Each contemplated the surprise encounter. "Who's your friend?"

"Hi, Sistie," Kathryn said, brightening, her surprise softened and dissipated by a wave of pride that Alana had come into the room. "This is Josh," she said haltingly, extending her arm out toward her visitor. "He's a friend from school."

Alana and Josh exchanged somewhat wary greetings, and then Alana retreated upstairs out of sight, but not out of earshot. She sat at the top of the stairs and eavesdropped on the conversation. Later that evening after Kathryn's friend had gone, Alana drifted into Kathryn's room.

"I'm proud of you, KK."

"What do you mean?"

"The way you handled Josh."

"Yeah, he's a good friend."

"Yeah, but, like, he was pressing you. Right?"

"Do you mean in the TV room?"

"Yeah, you know he was. You know he was pushing you a little bit. But I was proud of you, KK, because you resisted him."

Kathryn looked down, reflecting a mixture of guilt, pride, and embarrassment, but not questioning how Alana might have known this.

"But you know what he was after, right?" Alana asked. Kathryn looked away, uncertain as to what was behind the question. "Like, what do you think he wanted?"

Kathryn thought for a few moments looking to a spot somewhere toward the ceiling, above her and to the right, her finger on her protruding chin, searching her mind for possible answers.

"To touch me?"

"Yes, sweetie, exactly. He was pressing you, but you drew the line, and I'm proud of you."

Kathryn's posture straightened up, and she smiled.

The next day, Alana drew a figure on a page for Kathryn.

"Do you know what this is?" she asked Kathryn.

"Looks like a heart," Kathryn said as she stared at Alana's drawing.

"These are fallopian tubes," Alana said, pointing at two channels drawn on the page. She shaded in the pocket in the drawing where the tubes met. "Every month your body sends an egg from one or another of your ovaries—that's where the eggs are made— into one of these tubes."

Kathryn stared at the drawing. She thought for a minute. "You mean like chickens?"

"No, KK. These are super tiny little specs, but if they are fertilized by having sex with a boy, you will get pregnant." Kathryn drew her head back and stared at Alana. "And that could change your life forever."

* * *

Kathryn gradually traversed the period of repeated tachycardia episodes, and as they fell away, her medications were suspended. She seemed to have made it through the danger period.

During that time, even while I worried that Alana was struggling with the demands of her siblings, I begged for her help. I had leaned on her, ignoring the unfolding of her petals into the maturing rose. I became part of the crimping forces in her life, the forces that hemmed her in, that kept her from reaching out, taking risks, being free from the responsibilities of a caretaker. Only in retrospect did I see how much she was already doing, and in equal proportion, how much less I needed to do as a father for the kids, and how much more I could have given her.

BASEBALL AND STEINBECK
WITH ERIC

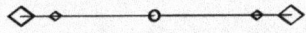

One summer, I took Eric to a minor league baseball game. The Frederick Keys team was playing the Durham Bulls. In the sixth inning, the action came close to us but it wasn't baseball.

Baseball

Four seats away, a boy about Eric's age began to raise a fuss with his father. He flailed about, his arms like a windmill, his voice loud, his words disrespectful. The boy was like that TiltA-Whirl without a horn. Eric sat staring, unbelieving. His eyes darted up to me and then back.

The boy left his seat and crossed in front of us, jostling us in our seats as we made way for him to pass along our row. Soon, back he came from left to right moving clumsily in front of us, his eyes focused on his father, paying no attention to the minor collisions he had with us. As he approached his father, he threw a punch at his dad's leg, screaming something unintelligible.

Eric stiffened, his face petrified, unmoving, eyes wide. He

looked as though he'd never seen someone act this way. He looked at me again. I met his eyes. Eric had been having his own outbursts toward Kathryn. The boy's outburst must have given Eric a new perspective.

"What happened? Why is he so angry?" Eric asked in a low voice.

"It's more than anger, Eric," I replied, trying to be calm, keeping my voice low. Both of us were absorbed in the commotion. "The boy may have a condition called autism," I said, glancing down to Eric and then again at the boy. "He has a hard time; his feelings are like a Tilt-A-Whirl. He doesn't know how to manage them." Eric sat up erect, eyes riveted on the boy. "The world is sometimes scary to him. He lashes out without understanding." Eric stared up at me, probing for meaning. I continued. "It's something he's born with."

After a pause, Eric asked "You mean like Kathryn?"

"No, Eric." I searched for words. "Kathryn was healthy when she was born. Then she caught a virus, an infection that attacked her heart and caused some brain damage." I studied Eric's face. "Autistic children are born wired a little differently than the rest of us."

Eric looked up into my eyes. I could see his anxiety begin to distort his face; moisture formed in his eyes.

The boy threw his baseball mitt at his father, then knocked over a cup of Coke. He was yelling loudly, and the entire section of the stadium was now watching the boy unleash his fury. The father—in my mind a paragon of steadiness, someone I admired—calmly picked up the boy, who was thrashing and screaming, and carried him to the nearest exit.

The father's patience was a model for me. His reaction was muted; he wasn't flustered or embarrassed. He looked like he had been dealing with this for a long time.

I imagined that Eric was internalizing the scene and comparing it with his own tantrums. The exaggerated public version of his own acting-out seemed to shake him. He sank in his seat. I think he began to see himself differently, at once more troubled and scared. His look of alarm melted into a sadness. He fell silent. He grabbed my arm and nestled up to me.

"Let's go, Daddy."

I tried to calm Eric on the drive home. "Some children are so very unlucky, Eric." He sat quietly next to me. "You too have been hit hard with your hearing loss. I know it's hard for you sometimes, too, isn't it?" Eric stared at the dashboard, then began to tear up again.

"Yes, Daddy," he said, looking up at me, his lip curled, his eyes filled with tears. "But I don't want to be like that."

Steinbeck.

A half-year later, while I was driving Eric home from school, he began to talk about a homework assignment, Steinbeck's *Of Mice and Men*. Eric devoured books, and his reading had already taken him near to the end of the book but hadn't yet reached the climax. My cloud of well-being began to darken. The main character, George, in Steinbeck's story ran a close parallel to Eric.

Like George, the big brother-like caretaker to the mentally troubled giant, Lennie, Eric had played the role of dependable helper and protector of Kathryn. The relationship had grown burdensome for Eric in his early years. She would incessantly pester Eric with questions and appeals for help. Eric would put a lid on his anger, but sometimes would blow up, such as the time he shouted at her, "Stop using my brain!"

The heartbreaking climax of the story *Of Mice and Men* was about to crash upon him. George's mercy killing of Lennie would have been a catastrophic moment for Eric. The story epitomized Kathryn's critical dependence on Eric. He was still struggling to come to terms with his sister's disabilities, not to mention his own. When Eric mentioned Lennie, I pulled over to the curb.

He had reached the point in the book where Lennie had accidentally killed the farmer's wife, and his revenge was looming. I twisted up inside. How to tell Eric about the way Lennie was going to meet his end? And how to square up the tricky imbalance in fates with Eric's own protection of Kathryn? How do you break the news to Eric about a protector whose only remedy to preserve a dream of a good life together with his friend is to shoot him from behind?

As I switched off the engine, I said, "Eric, there's something we need to talk about."

Puzzlement crept into his face. I drew in a deep breath, screwing up my courage.

"It's about the story you're reading, E." I paused to gather my thoughts. "You are about to run into a very nasty surprise in the story, and I think I should tell you a little bit about it." He turned more squarely toward me, to see my face from in front and to catch the whole message. "What do you think of George and Lennie?" I asked.

"He's taking care of Lennie. Lennie has a lot of problems."

"Remind you of anybody we know?"

"Kathryn?"

"And you," I paused. "A lot of the time you are like George, right? You step in to help her out, right?" He nodded and waited. "Even when you don't want to." Eric's face deepened in thought. My heart was in my throat again, just like when I had to tell Alana about her grandfather's death.

I explained to him that George felt he had to shoot Lennie to keep him from a worse fate at the hands of the farmer. I struggled mightily to keep my voice steady. My throat clogged up at the thought of the mercy killing.

Eric was speechless. He moped sullenly the entire day. He seemed to be trying to wrap his mind around the fate of Lennie. Years later, when he was an adult, and we were remembering those times, he said: "There was no way to really describe it, other than just an empty space searching for a light of meaning somewhere in there."

That was one piece of sky that I could see breaking off. Seeing it coming, I could at least soften the landing. It was a rare occasion, like Castaneda's observation that you often see leaves falling but never catch sight of the moment one breaks free from the twig. At least I caught sight of this one early. It was partly a reach skyward in protection, and partly a small success in catching a heavy emotion and talking it through.

Rolling discoveries about Eric led to constantly morphing challenges to my fathering. I found that as I came to grips with each emerging aspect of Eric's difficulties—in hearing, auditory processing, attention deficits, executive functioning, ostracism—I was always a step or more behind in my ability to offer support. The same held true for Kathryn and Alana. There is nothing static about fathering.

THE DIGNITY OF RISK

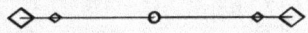

In 1997, when Kathryn was sixteen, I began to talk to Kathryn about Project Independence.

"What do you mean?" she asked.

"Well, Kathryn, one day you will want to live by yourself. You know Mom and Dad are not going to be around forever, and you will have to handle things on your own."

Kathryn looked down.

"Can I take my driving test?"

"I don't think you'll be able to drive as much as you want to," I said.

She frowned. All of us had been working on Kathryn about driving. It was out of the question. Even if she did pass a written test, her spatial perception and short-term memory issues would conspire against her.

"But just think, Kathryn, you won't have to worry about buying a car, buying gas, buying insurance. All of those things cost a lot of money." She looked back, blankly. "Besides, you are a whizz on the metro. And you can use a taxi anytime you need to get around."

Kathryn brightened a bit.

"And you'll have to learn how to handle money. You already have a bank account, and we'll show you how to write checks." Kathryn looked confused. "The main thing is to handle money, Kathryn. You have to carry around only as much as you need in your pocket every day. And keep track of how much you spend." Kathryn's wallet bulged with every single identification card and receipt she had collected. Our routine suggestions to slim down never made a dent.

Sorting through her pile of obsolete cards and papers, I often thought of squatters I had interviewed when on mission for the World Bank. Desperate for any small sign of recognition of being a person, worthy of respect, vulnerable to setbacks from many directions, they kept many small symbolic items of formal, sometimes bureaucratic recognition, like ID cards, credit cards, utility bills, and social security cards even if they were out of date or obsolete. As she grew into adolescence and began to perceive some of her limitations, I thought Kathryn kept cards, receipts, and every scrap of paper for similar reasons.

The big question Kathryn kept coming back to was, "What do you mean when you're 'not around'?" Kathryn had only a vague understanding of death.

A few years after Project Independence began, a friend was swept away in a flash flood. His body was found a few days later. That loss, her first confrontation with human mortality, shocked Kathryn. The prospect of not having her parents around gradually seeped in. We assured her and her siblings that we were determined to provide for her. We set up a trust and wills, but none of the stuff—trusts and legal protections—was easy for her to understand. Still, we repeated the ideas of Project Independence once or twice a month for a couple of years.

* * *

In their teen years, the kids became more independent, more mobile—and more exposed to the outside world. This exposure created new fatherhood challenges.

One particularly acute moment came on a family cruise in the Mediterranean in the summer of 1998. Alana was twenty, Kathryn nearing seventeen, and Eric fourteen. While at sea, Kathryn wanted to go to the ship's small disco after dinner.

"Dad, can I go up by myself?" she asked. Linda and I exchanged glances. How can we say no to a winsome young lady eager to try her wings? The boat wasn't gigantic. Our cabin was only two decks away. Some of the crew knew her. Would they be reliable chaperones in disguise?

"Kathryn, what if you get lost? How will you find your way back?" we queried. She knew she had many problems orienting herself in space. She would get lost often on bike paths, ski trails, even in her middle school hallways between classes. Linda had put up colored tape on the walls when she first started school to help her remember where to go. Or whenever she would get lost out on the street, I would often get a phone call. She would tell me the intersection, but we sank into confusion about location and orientation. She couldn't tell which direction she should go next.

"And you know you can't drink because of your heart

condition." All of this was the nervousness of parents conditioned by years of dealing with disabilities. We drew some deep breaths.

My instinct was to hold her back. I fought the ghosts of past seizures, a compromised heart, disorientation in space, and meeting the wrong guy. I reminded her of the previous summer. She had given her credit card to a new friend who promptly ran up nearly two thousand dollars in charges.

I searched my mind for small hints and subtle signals that she was ready to take on something new. Her sleepaways at summer camps the previous years? My watchman's cap was on, and I stared directly into a mirror, asking myself if I was ready to defy my instinct to hold her back.

Eric, sitting in our stateroom on the periphery of our conversation, cocked his head and turned up his palms as if to say, "Come on, Dad." He mouthed, "Time to take the risk."

Kathryn touched up her rouge, put on new earrings, and set off with a kiss and a hug. Part of my heart went with her out the cabin door and down the passageway.

We fidgeted nervously in our stateroom for nearly an hour. Finally, the anxiety got the better of me. I needed to see how she would fare. I worried that Kathryn the innocent could walk in front of a freight train she didn't see. Despite her high social IQ, I needed to see how she would handle the situation on her own—the pressures exerted by her peers, the temptations offered by older guys. Would she end up back in some stranger's cabin?

I caught sight of her in the pulsing blue light over the small dance floor. The undulating bodies made it hard to get a clear view. She stood alone in white blouse and brown skirt gazing somewhere toward the ceiling as the dancers gyrated around her. She had a familiar expression of puzzlement and promise. More than a couple of guys circled around on the periphery, nervously chatting with each other, staring at their drinks, rolling up their sleeves, glancing occasionally at Kathryn. Sooner or later, one by one, each guy came to focus on the one standing there in puzzlement.

I was probably the only guy in the room that didn't have designs on my daughter. I wasn't there just for protection. I was unable to beat back a curiosity about how she would do out on her own. She had a lifetime of proving herself to be a fighter and an achiever. But could she survive out in the open? Most people would consider these to be safe surroundings—a disco on a small cruise ship. I could only think of the place as a shark tank. Maybe it could be a good testing ground.

I laid back outside the perimeter of the disco crowd, so as not to be seen. Certain that Kathryn was unaware of my presence, I was subjecting myself, and her, to a reality check. To the overprotective dad who had spent the first five years of her life keeping her alive, was I now keeping her from living? The scene on the disco floor was gut-wrenching.

Kathryn stood alone, almost forlorn. The tunes rolled out like thunder. Though affable, she wasn't the type to strike up a conversation with strangers. Besides, her hearing impairment put her at a large disadvantage in noisy environments. She had taken up a spot on the edge of the dance floor, her arm resting on a shelf, putting herself out there for the world to see. The scene was turning into more than a reality check. It was becoming a test for Dad. All I could see was vulnerability. A half-dozen younger guys saw a sweet image dying to be on the dance floor.

A tall young man, eighteen or nineteen, stepped forward and extended his hand. He said something to her. I hoped she could hear it. The throbbing music and a multitude of raised voices made it impossible to hear anything. The pair took the floor together among a dozen other couples. She looked self-conscious, avoiding eye contact with her partner. Her rhythm was off, her hips and shoulders out of sync with the rest of her body. She was following a beat no one else in the room was hearing. Kathryn was a great swimmer and could jump rope for hours, but her sense of rhythm was jumbled up. But she was there. She was game, holding her own, dancing her dance, being a part of the crowd.

One by one, the dance partners dwindled away. Kathryn ended up back at her spot, alone and waiting. Maybe she couldn't keep the conversation going. Maybe she didn't *hear* the conversation. Only a few guys hung back, drinking near the bar. My protective instincts surged toward the surface, but I was becoming conspicuous and felt, for her dignity's sake, that I should leave.

* * *

Our stateroom door shut with a soft thud. It was well past midnight. Kathryn wasn't great at slipping in unnoticed. Not that it mattered. Linda and I were staring at the ceiling in the dark, awaiting her return.

I let a few minutes pass as she settled in the room.

"How did it go, honey?" I asked nervously in the dark. My anxieties were still swirling.

"Fine," she said, drawing out the 'ine' in a soft, vague way. "A little bit weird."

"What do you mean 'weird'?"

"You usually go to a disco with somebody, right? Being alone reminded me of camp."

"You mean the at Camp Rimrock?" I asked, my heart sinking. "When you couldn't bear for us to leave?"

"No, no, no, not that one. I mean Camp Summit . . . the one after Rimrock." A silence followed. I quickly thought back. Kathryn had attended a camp in her twelfth year and was recruited as a helper to the athletic instructor. She took attendance and demonstrated sports games. "It was weird then too. I mean, like, when I had to start my job."

"You're talking about the assistant's job?"

"Yeah. That one. It was like having to be out there again, by myself, giving demonstrations. It was hard then in a new job, trying to know what to do." Another pause. "Only this time, tonight, I knew what to do. I could handle it."

I slept well that night, dropping off with a smile on my face. The anxiety from earlier in the evening was completely gone, but not the chagrin. I wrestled a little inside, trying to persuade my Phantom to loosen up. Time to take some risks, indeed. And Eric had called the shot. Fatherhood was moving away from being too careful, toward learning how to take risks.

RIBBONS ON WAYPOINTS

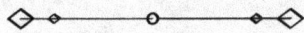

The scene of Eric's high school graduation could have been a movie set. A thousand family members gathered in a lovely spring afternoon at an outdoor amphitheater surrounded by tall beeches and oaks. The graduating class of boys sat on stage, decked out in khakis and blue blazers. A buzz of anticipation filled the air. Tiers of seats for parents and family rose from the stage to the top rim.

Though it was a time for celebration, we came with a certain melancholy. The previous evening, awards for academic and other achievements had been handed out. Most of Eric's friends and many others received honors for drama, athletics, scholarship, citizenship, and a half-dozen other categories. Although he was the only one of his group who had not received an award that night, Eric put on a brave face. "Those guys deserved the ones they got," he said.

The reality is that he had battled through many head winds and shined in ways we hadn't anticipated, in academics, drama, singing, and sports. But accolades and supportive cheering outside our family didn't always accompany his accomplishments.

At the graduation, the headmaster stepped to the microphone and broke into the rock music playing over the loudspeakers. As the music died down he said, "We have the most important awards still to issue."

Heads in the audience lifted, chatter died away. He mentioned the highest-ranking scholar and a few outstanding college admissions. Applause followed the winners to their seats.

"Now I want to turn to an award that has been part of our school for decades." The crowed fell silent. Linda and I were standing at the uppermost rim of the arena. We surveyed the crowd, still feeling a little empty, eyes focused on Eric in one moment, then sweeping around the gathering the next.

"This award is presented to the Sixth Former [senior] who has most clearly demonstrated the qualities of fearlessness and tenacity of purpose," he said.

"This year's recipient is a school 'lifer,' having come to the school as a third grader in 1994. Throughout his career with us, he has demonstrated precisely the kind of fearlessness that this award celebrates. He is a risk-taker. Academically, he has never shied away from the most demanding academic courses, even if they haven't always played to his strengths. He chose to wrestle each winter for all four years in the upper school, although he never qualified to wrestle in a varsity match."

The "risk-taker" comment caught my attention and piqued my curiosity. I thought of the many boys in the school who had tried new things—school newspaper, computer club. When he got to "wrestling," my ears perked up. Eric was a wrestler but never a starter. Then he mentioned that the award winner had "appeared in every major upper school production, although he's never been cast in a central role." That's when I knew he was headed for Eric. I began to tear up. My throat closed. I looked down again to Eric, but I couldn't detect any hint of knowing on his face. He sat in the front row of graduates, his head down, staring at the ground.

The headmaster continued. "Despite living with a hearing impairment, he actively performs in the school chorus and in the premier singing group. He's what theater people call a trouper. He clearly enjoys taking on challenges, trying his hand at something new, and extending the limits of his personal zone of comfort. Over the years, he has developed into an increasingly confident and self-assured young man, a good friend to his classmates, and tower of strength in the face of the inevitable obstacles. He has described his career at school as 'an ever-changing machine,' not so much characterized by the rigidity of metal, but by the tenacity of function and purpose.

"This young man does not know the meaning of defeat. Rather, he has persevered, he has endured, and he has flourished. His advisor says of this young man: 'He cares deeply about people and projects that draw people together. He will stop to assist those who are in greater need than he is, helping the younger student with his math, the inexperienced wrestler with a new move. He is supportive of his family, his friends, and his school.' This year I am pleased to present this special award to Eric Kent Campbell."

A thundering applause erupted immediately. His classmates gave him a standing ovation.

By the time he came to "he does not know the meaning of defeat," Linda and I were in tears and in each other's arms. *Fearlessness and tenacity of purpose,* I thought. Those words added new dimension to Eric, now seen in the eyes of the school community.

That was when we began to look around us and noticed that Eric's teachers and administrators were all focused on us, standing in a small pod in the rear of the amphitheater. They were all in the know. Not a word had leaked. They were poised to see our reaction. A professional videographer had his camera trained on us, capturing on video our surprise. Later, Eric's teachers told us that voting among the faculty was unanimous.

That recognition brought home something I should've cherished in Eric long before he graduated. He had a reputation for being straight up, for being brave, for always helping others first, for being the good guy, for having courage to fight through. Ever since I'd worn his hearing aids at Ocean City a decade earlier, I should have appreciated the fearlessness and tenacity, his lifelong fight to level the playing field. And risk-taking? Of course, he was taking risks every day, just being in there, trying, not turning away.

* * *

For Kathryn, completing high school was a monumental achievement, adorned by special recognition as well. Early in her middle school years, the prospect of even getting through the upper grades seemed daunting.

One night at dinner time, she came hurrying by me and

took a seat at the kitchen table. She had been struggling with her math problem.

"Oooh, I don't get it!"

"What's the matter, Kathryn?" I asked.

"I did these problems right yesterday," she replied, with a snap. "But they're not working today." She wasn't ready to accept help, and I returned to cutting onions. Kathryn pushed her chair away from the table and put her book down hard.

"I'm going to make something of myself," she declared loudly. I stopped in my tracks, stunned by her determination and self-awareness.

"Kathryn, that's a really good way to think about things. But I'm sorry you're feeling badly about your work."

Her eyes began to tear up. She laid her head down on her arm and fell quiet. I sat down beside her and put my arm on her shoulder. After a few minutes, she raised her head up and looked at me.

"Dad," she said in plaintively, "if I hadn't been sick, could I have gone to Yale?"

A bowling ball landed at the pit of my stomach. I swallowed hard, tried to look nonchalant and searched for words, masking my paralysis with a comforting hug. I had no idea she had gained so much perspective about her condition and her limitations. And I was surprised that she had picked up the idea of university, much less Yale, from conversations she must have overheard from her sister and her friends.

"Kathryn. Yes, if you hadn't been sick, you could have gone anywhere. The sky was the limit." She blinked at me, a hint of a smile crept onto her face with the imagined prospect, and then ran away as the reality settled in.

"Honey, even the doctors commented about how you lifted your eyes and looked around the room as a newborn." My words sank in again with positive effect, and again, soon evaporated.

She thought hard for a few moments. I could see her formulating a way out. "Well . . . will I get better?"

"Sweetie, you were hit by lightning. It's not something that can be reversed. It's not fair. You were very unlucky. A virus came out of the blue and attacked your heart. It also affected your brain. We thought we were going to lose you." She stared at a spot somewhere over my head, taking it in. "You know, other kids with the same virus didn't make it. Only you did."

Kathryn sat silently for a while, wrestling with these ideas: hit hard, but the only survivor. I studied her moistening eyes. She sighed, and a tension was released inside. Then I continued.

"But there are things that you can do about it." She lifted her chin a little higher. "Remember what your mother always tells you."

"What, to work hard?"

"Exactly. That and to make the most of what you have. You know, you have a really positive attitude. It's not just aptitude. You are doing amazingly well on these math problems, you're really good at vocabulary, you can remember things that most of us forget, and you can type with blazing speed."

Kathryn brightened. Then she looked down at her math problems and the scribbly sheet written on in pencil and erased a half-dozen times.

"Come on," I said. "Let's look at those problems one more time."

* * *

When she began to get beyond arithmetic, she got pretty good at factoring and later, began algebra. She could memorize the steps and after a while, recognize a pattern in the problem. She put hours of study into these skills, and eventually they paid off.

Her dedication to practice and studying is an attribute, much like her mother's, that's hardwired. Kathryn often commented at the end of the day that she "wanted to use up all her energy." She wanted to get everything out of life. She would play a computer typing game for hours. Later, this habit of practice showed up in an increasing speed on the keyboard. Her fingers flew across the tiny keys on phones and computers. Her practice worked with vocabulary as well. She loved the word-a-day calendars and she would memorize words. She loved trying them out on us.

"Dad, how did it go with your comrades today at work?"

As a World Bank guy, I thought that one especially amusing. Or she might say, "Dad, I hate to be vexing you, but would you help me with the problem again?"

Linda spent countless hours every day on Kathryn's homework, generating ideas that were catchy and attractive to keep her involved. Only when it came to creative enterprises of problem-solving, and later in expository writing and story-telling, did her natural energies and skills begin to falter.

Kathryn was buoyed by her success in her high school's special education program. We all were. Told in the beginning that she probably wouldn't graduate, we were amazed at the awards ceremony after her graduation. She received prizes for dedication, community service, the most improved, and even a Presidential Citation. Sitting there hearing her name called out in a vast auditorium spread a balm over all the past pain.

At that moment, I recalled the day she'd broken free from a crowd of soccer players and dribbled the length of a pitch to score her first goal. The awards were like that. We did a victory dance, too, over the false proposition that she might not graduate. Her victory was a testament to her mother, her siblings, the public education system, to the attention given even to disabled students, and most of all to Kathryn, who managed through her own internal drive and hard work to achieve something some thought was beyond her reach.

* * *

Both kids found a way to excel, not despite their disabilities, but partly because of them. They forged ways without having a model from me, even though certainly they were imbued with drive and benefited from a lot of hands-on help and extracurricular resources from their mom and me. I was the confidant, the problem-solver, resident writer, and backup to Linda. The kids came to trust me as a source of advice. But their achievements were singularly their own.

From the fatherly perspective, I saw small glimmers of the payoff for having cut free a little more from the cautions and conservatism my Phantom might have engendered. Payoff, also, from finding ways to engage in sensitive and scary topics like fears for Kathryn's future, her own concerns about college, Eric's fears about George and Lennie. These led to self-confidence and a willingness to face tough challenges. That built a level of trust that firmed up their psychological and emotional foundations. Linda deserved awards herself for heroic mothering, for never quitting, always searching for something extra to enrich the kids. But I can say also that some parts of the hybrid model—engaging emotionally and gaining trust—those parts worked, too.

PORTRAIT OF KATHRYN
AS A YOUNG WOMAN

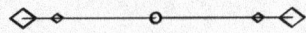

I never escaped the emotional sting when I had to remind Kathryn of her disabilities, which we boiled down to short-term memory, comprehension problems, and difficulty hearing. Yet she needed reminding from time to time, to understand why she couldn't do some things her friends did, like going to the beach together or driving a car. She showed recognition of her deficits, and gradually came to terms with them. Then, every once in a while, there was a surprising, sympathetic reminder for Dad.

"Dad," she inquired one day, "how are you feeling?" Her question was a little odd, like something suspiciously hidden, as though she were probing, knowing something I did not.

"Fine, Kathryn. Why do you ask?"

"I wondered how things were going. You know, it being a dolorous anniversary."

I smiled at Kathryn's "dolorous." But then I thought quickly to get the point of her question, clearing through the clutter of the day to see the wider sweep of meaning. Seeing me lost, she continued. "It's October 19, 2000. I'm sorry, Dad.

Your mom died a year ago, today."

The "disabled" one, the one with memory problems, was caring for me. I stood stunned for a few moments, opening my heart to meet hers. We hugged and wiped our tears.

On the other hand, she would ask with maddening regularity about the ordinary daily details. When do we leave? What is it we were about to do? What did we do yesterday? Long-term memory was a strength; short-term was an enduring difficulty.

* * *

Linda had been a chugging locomotive driving to find the best educational arrangements for Kathryn in her middle and high school years. She was determined to take Kathryn's formal learning as far as possible. Besides her education, Linda felt it important to widen her social contacts and help her develop a more normal life.

"Community college is the obvious next step for her," Linda announced one evening.

"That's not a step; it's a gigantic leap," I replied. I couldn't see a way for Kathryn to succeed, given her disabilities. "Think about damage of setting her up to fail," I said in a mildly accusatory tone.

Linda shot back, "The local community college has a good accommodations program," Linda said. "It's geared to jobs, not academics. She's a high school graduate. She can memorize steps in math and she loves to read. It's worth a try."

After weeks of debate, Linda arranged for Kathryn to

take the entrance exam to a community college. Kathryn was excited about this prospect. It might not be Yale, but it was a college. This was something grand, an idea that brightened Kathryn's eyes. An idea that I felt had been demolished by that virus.

On the day of the exam, Kathryn was nervous, but game. Linda coached her on testing strategy.

"Remember Kathryn, try to eliminate the obvious wrong answers. If you don't know the answer, just move on to the next question."

"What if I can't answer any?"

"Don't worry, you will know some answers, and you can guess at others or skip them. Remember to eliminate the obvious wrong ones."

"Uh, OK…. yeah, I'll try to remember," she said haltingly, her face a little blank. I was not at all sure she would get through the first page, much less the entire test.

A week after the test, the envelope from the community college came in the mail. It was on the table when I arrived home from work. We gathered around and delivered it to Kathryn to open. There was much anticipation. Kathryn stared at the computer-generated message.

"I got a seven," she said.

We thought for a minute. Seven.

"What about the percentile, Kathryn? What was the total? Was it ten?" we asked.

Linda looked at the paper. Her face fell. "It's out of one hundred," she said dryly. "She needed to get fifty to gain admission. She got seven."

Kathryn fought hard to keep the tears away. We all did. They pushed themselves out just the same. We hugged and comforted her, all of us weeping awkwardly, the whole family one big blob of tears. Eric and Alana were crestfallen for their sister. Linda and I needed hugs too, not just for consolation. I felt like I had to suppress my anger. No one really needed any more proof of Kathryn's disabilities, and here we were party to putting the evidence in black and white right there in front of her.

I felt yanked back to reality, slapped harshly across the face with facts contrary to my hopes, my willingness to ignore or forget Kathryn's disabilities, my wishful thinking that she might somehow succeed on her splinter skills and ability to remember steps in arithmetic.

I recalled the psychologist who remarked one day after testing her that Kathryn presented a deceiving picture. She looked, behaved, and functioned at a much higher level than she actually was. She was polite, affable, and had a sunny disposition. We were lulled into the notion that Kathryn was doing better. Now we felt the cold spray of reality once again.

* * *

Months later, Linda discovered a remedial program offered by the community college for students whose scores were too low to qualify for admission. A few of Kathryn's friends were in the same boat, although none was quite as challenged as Kathryn. Space was limited. Linda talked with the moms, and they all resolved to show up at the college to sign up for the class.

On sign-up day, Linda was up and dressed at four-thirty a.m. She was on the campus when the janitors arrived to open the doors. The security guard wanted to usher her away, but she refused to budge. She was the first in line and had been waiting for three hours when the clerk lifted the customer window to take inquiries.

The test preparedness program was to run over the summer months. It was a self-paced, computerized program, but students had to be in the college lab to progress. Every weekend, Linda would sit with Kathryn to review her work, coaching her, showing her how to figure out the questions, marking the answers and then reacting to the feedback generated automatically by the computer program. With each advance in level of accomplishment, the questions would get slightly harder, and students would have to maintain their level of skill; otherwise, they would fall back to the previous, simpler level. With Linda's help, Kathryn progressed upward several levels. The next week, she would find that Kathryn had fallen back a level or more.

During one weekend session at home, Kathryn's fingers flew on the keyboard, tapping out a paragraph in a few minutes. Her narrative was comprehensible, but it contained many repetitions and side comments that interrupted the flow. She would print out her homework and hand it to Linda. I sat nearby, observing.

Linda said, "Kathryn, you really batted this out fast."

"I know, right?" Kathryn replied. "I can type almost 100 words per minute."

"But you have to work on not saying the same thing over and over." Linda pointed out three sentences that basically said the same thing.

"Oh...yeah, I get it," Kathryn replied slowly.

* * *

Every weekday, Kathryn would walk to the metro, catch a train to the station nearest the campus, walk to catch a bus, and finally arrive on campus to start her session. It took her an hour each way. This she did every weekday for ten weeks. Gradually, Kathryn's scores lifted several levels above the starting place. She had worked diligently. Besides the daily trips, she handed in homework, which consisted of worksheets she would produce while on the computer, in addition to short essays and stories that were meant to complement her work.

At last, Kathryn completed the program. She felt a sense of accomplishment. She was enchanted with the idea of having been working on a college campus, even though her work wasn't actually on college material. Going to the campus, mixing with students, and eating in the cafeteria seemed to give her a lift. She was preparing, participating, advancing. Her attitude seemed to show that she was making something of herself and began to see herself in a new light. She was seeing evidence that she wasn't shut out completely from higher education. Her spirits were up and so were ours. At the conclusion of the program, the participants once again took the admission test.

About two weeks later, a letter arrived from the college inviting Kathryn and us to a session with the summer program administrators to discuss the results of her admission score. Linda was tied up with patients, so I went with Kathryn. We were nervous entering the waiting room in the program counseling area. At last, Kathryn was called.

Two people faced us, a man and a woman, both middle-aged and serious. They sat across a table from us. The room seemed cavernous and had the feeling of an interrogation center. I explained my accompanying Kathryn.

The man started. "Kathryn, how did you feel about the test?" He paused while Kathryn turned her focus to him. "Do you have trouble usually when you take tests?" he asked.

My mouth went dry. Kathryn did not seem to perceive the foreboding in the question.

"Not usually," she swallowed. "I do pretty well," she replied in a halting manner, but in a way that projected total candor.

"I see," he replied.

The lady stepped in. "Kathryn, did you have any particular difficulty with the test?"

"No, well, yes. I mean, it took me a long time, but I thought I got through most of the questions." Kathryn rolled her hands forward in a gesture to suggest moving through something.

Then the man again. "Kathryn. We would like to show you the results." He began walking his fingers through a sheaf of papers. "Here they are," he said, after peering down and picking out several pieces of paper which he laid before us on the desk.

"On June 17, you scored a seven on the test. That is far from the fifty you need to gain admission to the college." I could see Kathryn stiffen her back as the oral report came rolling out. "And here," he continued, "August 7 is your last score. It is an eight."

My heart sank. Kathryn didn't reveal her reaction, but I sensed she was collapsing inside as well. I touched her back in a small hidden gesture of support. Her face grew long, her eyes turned down, a tear dropped on her dress.

"Tell me this, Kathryn," said the lady. "What is your goal at the community college?"

Kathryn seemed to rally a bit, as if she saw an opportunity to talk about her dreams. After a brief pause, she began, "I really want to go into early childhood education." She paused again, and then began to warm up. "I love working with kids. I worked as a counselor at camp, and in a bridge program. I want to be able to teach in preschool or early elementary." I got the feeling that Kathryn would roll on for another fifteen minutes about her work history and dreams. Her delivery was smooth, her eyes widening, little bits of enthusiasm danced on her words, but she drew up short, seeing the two administrators exchange glances. The man nodded affirmatively and held up a hand.

"There is something more to the test results, Kathryn." He pointed to two stacks of papers sitting on his desk. "You see this stack of papers, here?"

Kathryn followed his indication to a small pile of papers. "This is the accumulation of homework turned in by all the other students in your summer class." He then moved another pile into a central position on his desk. "This stack, three times higher than the others, is your homework."

A smile of pride broke over Kathryn, her lip peeled out, half in smile, half in tears.

"And there is this," said the administrator. "You registered 287 hours on the computer during the summer." He pointed to a chart in his file. "The average for the students this summer was less than ninety." He looked at his colleague and then back to Kathryn. "You have shown a very high level of motivation and hard work."

Then I piped in, unable to resist. "I think you should know that Kathryn doesn't drive a car. She has to walk to the metro, ride to the nearest station, then catch a bus to get here. It took a lot of effort."

Another glance between the two. Then the man said: "Kathryn, we have written a letter to the administration recommending that you be admitted under special waivers and on probation effective this fall. You will have to maintain a C average or better. Are you still interested in attending the community college?"

I felt a burst inside, my heart flooded with excitement, relief, and joy. I wasn't embarrassed that laughter and tears were flowing freely. Kathryn and I gulped and hugged and flustered in front of the administrators. On sheer grit and with her mother's help, Kathryn had plucked forward, using every bit of her energy to make something of herself. I felt surprisingly lost at that moment. My dream fatherhood project was little more than a shadowy memory. Life was happening. It hardly seemed that fatherhood was the same. I was more like a partner. I was bursting with pride for Kathryn and in deep admiration of her mother.

A PIECE OF THE FALLEN SKY

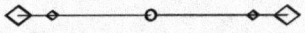

A year after his college graduation in 2010, I proposed to Eric that we attend the annual meeting of the American Association for the Advancement of Science in San Diego. I knew from having attended past AAAS meetings in my graduate school days that the events offer lots of stimulation to someone ready for the next phase of life. The 2010 program scheduled many sessions on policy and practice in energy use and environmental change, Eric's areas of study at university. I saw our excursion as a way to deepen our bond, plus the trip gave me an opportunity to offer guidance in the next phase of his life. But the biggest impact of the trip was not bonding or trust. Rather, a big fat piece of the sky fell right in my lap. In the rubble, I found I was right about the bonding, but the guidance bit flowed in the opposite direction to the one I expected.

I selected an inn across the bay from the conference center. The secluded place gave Eric and me plenty of one-on-one time. On the fourth morning, still in our hotel room making ready to head for the conference center, Eric came near the bathroom where I was shaving.

He announced in a reprimanding tone, "That was really bad, Dad."

I looked at myself in the mirror, rapidly going over the events of the morning, searching for any bumpiness or tension, maybe something I did at breakfast or during the previous night?

I had rarely heard this tone from Eric and hardly ever directed at me. "Yesterday, at the jobs booth," he continued. A realization crept slowly over me that I had somehow screwed up, but I couldn't pinpoint it.

An emotional wave passed over me. It started as a small tremor in my core, but then I diverted my attention to the details of shaving, to buy time, making the razor swaths overlap. But the disturbance was inescapable. I finished up in front of the mirror.

"It was really bad, Dad," he said again, his hands now on his hips.

The tremor grew stronger. I stepped away from the sink, toweling off, searching my mind for the problem. Then it struck me: the booth we visited the previous day. I had begun to chat up representatives of a research center at their jobs booth. I had worked for a couple of years at one of the agencies represented at the booth and started speaking to the people there more or less bilaterally, leaving Eric out of the loop.

"I ... I had worked at one of those jobs early in my career, Eric. I know their mission. You would be a good fit."

"You have to leave it to me, Dad."

"I'm sorry, Eric," but I didn't really look him in the eye. I began to realize that I had crossed a line. A flush of guilt warmed my cheeks.

"You have to let me do it. I'll figure it out."

"I was only trying to help, Eric. I lost sight of how they might have seen you."

Eric scowled at me.

I had failed to discern the boundary hidden in all the fuzziness that lies between a father and a gifted son with disabilities. The fuzziness, like Spanish moss, had grown slowly, persistently, but unnoticed ever since discovering Eric's hearing loss. In a way, I had become disabled, too. Unable to perceive his needs clearly, I never knew how or whether to intervene. Offer too much help, you worry about usurping his prerogatives; offer too little, you worry he will flounder.

I had stepped too far. Worse, I had put him back into little boyhood. He made me see it. I thought I had succeeded in many ways, yet ended up failing Eric by overdoing it. The realization struck me like hammer blow. I plunged into full-throated sobs. The scene took me back sharply to my own father's breakdown when my brother and I were in our mid-teens.

* * *

"One of the worst things you can do," Dad had said flatly. "Getting a girl pregnant is wrong in so many ways," Dad blurted out his warning like a wannabe deacon, stiff and uncomfortable. His statements came out of the blue and not for any particular reason other than Kent and I were growing into early manhood. He sat at our kitchen table. My brother and I, fifteen and thirteen, stood in the room across the table from him like two passersby, roped in as a captive audience, unprepared for what seemed like a compulsory message. Mom stood apart at the far end of the kitchen, more or less keeping her distance. Kent told me later he was sure Mom had urged Dad to give us early adolescents "the lecture." Kent and I stood awkwardly near the table, not wanting to sit, wary of engaging too much.

"I know, Dad," I offered, glancing nervously at Kent for support.

"It's a sin, one of the worst," Dad continued. We nodded to acknowledge his message but without knowing what to say. It was a pronouncement, not a conversation.

Dad cleared his throat. That was a sign. It wasn't a cough, but a clearing sound, which always signaled a seriousness. No phlegm-clogged break should be allowed to interfere or raise doubt about the gravity of the moment. But Dad wasn't good at this guidance-giving stuff. He was putting on a little extra volume. The sheriff in the house was dictating the law without any triggering event, without breaking any ice, forget about developing any rapport. He was trying to cram a giant moral lesson of the times into a couple of sentences.

Kent and I shuffled our feet while making vague gestures of agreement with Dad. Mom held her position at the end of the kitchen, letting Dad do the heavy lifting.

In fact, we agreed completely with Dad. Truth was, I was years away from my first sexual encounter and, frankly, I didn't know that much about my brother's sex life. We didn't discuss our girlfriends in that way. For one thing, we were more than two years apart in age. For another, because rapid growth in our suburban area forced boundary changes in schools, we ended up going to different high schools and had few friends in common.

After an extended pause, Dad fell silent, his message delivered, important, but flat, like a billboard. Dad's motives were right, but the only thing decidedly not pregnant was the moment. He failed to connect with us, and he knew it.

Even at thirteen, I suspected that Dad's skill at schmoozing about the rules of life were stunted by growing up without his father around. Dad was right to address the topic, right about needing to give my brother and me fatherly guidance, but he had fallen out of touch with his boys.

Then, seemingly having perceived the gap that had opened up between us, Dad blurted out, "I've tried." His voice began to break. I froze at this deepening. "I've tried to be a good father," his voice rose. A sob burst out, he gasped for air. "Maybe it's because I've been away too much," he said, haltingly, in tears. Kent and I stood paralyzed.

My father realized—we all did—that years of professional travel had robbed him and his two boys of a bonding that can only come with the friction of life, working in close quarters, dealing with conflict. My father's outburst came in staccato fashion, as though he struggled internally to allow his emotions to the surface. The tears and sobs overrode all else. Neither Kent nor I found a way to harness the moment and convert it into a turning point. Instead, the moment passed, our masks of stiff exterior morphed into ones of meek sympathy. Dad's teary outburst then was in recognition of a loss much like I was seeing now at the science conference with Eric: Fathers out of touch, getting caught by surprise or blindly reaching for the sky when nothing was falling.

* * *

Fortunately for me, Eric may have been injured by my clumsy attempt to speak for him at the science conference, but he was plenty man enough to see the remorse in my tears. He did something I wish I could have done for my father.

"C'mon, Dad," Eric said as he put his arms around me. "Let's hug it out."

Eric seemed to have caught a glimpse of the faults in his father he hadn't seen before and stepped in to make up the difference. Instead of me, the steady one, the one who had always found the solution, the paternal redoubt, Eric saw a crack in his father's shell and stepped forward smoothly to patch the gap.

Only then did another subtle color of my hybrid model of fathering begin to glow. I realized that dads don't always have to deliver solutions. Sometimes it's enough to hint or suggest. At the jobs booth, an introduction would have been enough. As I learned from Eric in San Diego, and on other occasions, that's all there was to being a hero.

During our "hugging it out," Eric seemed to perceive the roots of my protectiveness, even though he couldn't yet be aware that his father's blundering over the fuzzy line originated decades earlier when the sky seemed to be drawing nearer to his sick sister. Twenty-five years earlier, the impulse hold up the sky was as natural and unpretentious as a caveman feeling a flood of adrenaline. It would lead many times to inappropriate, if innocent, intrusions on my part into Eric's process of becoming. Now, in his strong embrace, I caught a glimpse of a man budding before my very eyes, taking the mantle easily into his own hands and carrying it gracefully forward.

With this ease of transition, I learned something unexpected in the accidental meteorology of falling sky. The pieces aren't hard or brittle. Quite surprisingly, they are soft, malleable, and they almost always end up being moist. For each piece of sky came a corresponding clump of heart, exposed, sometimes scarred from having been buried too long. And, most of all, picking up a piece of fallen sky wasn't a period at the end of a long sentence of decay, but rather a conjunction into something new. The pieces can be massaged and shaped. Eric and I squeezed a great big piece between us, and as it became a thing of bonding, a small bit of glue, a foundation of trust. That experience shifted my defensive posture a few degrees. I became a little less defensive, a little more able to see the Phantom in his subtle camouflage.

My kids, who were already racing ahead in developing their own means to shape the world, were dealing with pieces of the sky on their own. They were fending for themselves and I had just missed the signals. I was so wrapped up in my worry and concern, always looking ahead, worried that Alana wouldn't finish her education or that Eric would not be able to pull through university or graduate school. So worried that I missed the new, soft, green edges of growth that were already sprouting from them. I began to feel less worried about pieces of the fallen sky; I saw that the whole enterprise of skyholding was obsolete. It might have been helpful in the big bang of the family following Kathryn's illness, but the kids' growth had long ago outpaced any powers I might have had to keep the sky in place.

A CHRISTMAS STORY

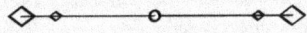

When I left Berkeley in 1988 to move to Washington, DC, and take a job at the World Bank, I imagined that besides eliminating our medical debts, I would develop a fat Rolodex at the end of five years, and that would set me up with consulting contacts for a long time. Now, twenty-five years later, I was finally back in Berkeley. Linda stayed temporarily in Bethesda, while Kathryn and I formed an advance team to scout out our new old home. We pulled up to the house in a rented car for the first time in twenty-five years not as just visitors.

I thought of the many times I had visited our block, stopping over in San Francisco on my way to Asia or somewhere. I would stay in our neighbor's house across the street and stare out the second-story window at my house, rented to someone else, warm lights showing through the windows, wondering when I would ever return.

A deep emotional tug drew me back. There was life business to finish. Kathryn and I shared the same psychological and emotional pull to return to our Berkeley house where so much good and bad had begun. I had a deep longing to be there again, to return to the scene where our lives had been so dreamy, then so interrupted by crisis, so chaotic in the children's early lives. Perhaps I could master our fate by returning to where we had started, to pick up the dream once again.

We ascended the thirty-six steps to the front door, opened all the windows to let light and fresh air inside. We entered in a quiet revery and silently walked from room to room, taking it in like astronauts on a distant planet revisiting after a long absence. We wandered about inside without uttering a word. Our excursion brought many memories flooding back.

Finally, I sat at the kitchen table where I'd begun the journey two-and-a-half decades earlier. In my mind, I ran through a summary of my life. The wonderful house on Domingo we thought would be our last, the health threats and heartaches, the move to Chevy Chase, its convivial neighborhood filled with warm neighbors and tall trees, a great professional career and, at last, after all those years, I was back. I slapped the table with my hands and rose to my feet, asking myself out loud, "Now, where was I?"

All in all, our deck had been shuffled many times, but the house weathered the years well, and being together in this dignified old place afforded a sense of continuity and completion. A few days after arriving, Alana, Eric, and I were on the phone together.

"What's it like, Dad?" Alana asked.

"So amazing, honey." I paused to gather my thoughts. When we left the Berkeley house in 1988, we had just completed a major addition and Alana was ten years old.

"Alana, you know we left the house entirely furnished, right? Down to the books, art, the stereo, TV, dishes."

"I remember," she replied. "You even left those Marimekko curtains in my bedroom."

"It's a time warp. Everything's still here. Just like we left it."

"Wow, amazing."

"Except the Marimekkos. They're pretty faded."

"But how does it feel?" Eric inquired.

I recounted the memories about the years of friends, neighbors, and professional life in Washington, followed by the scene at the kitchen table upon my return—the slap of the table and the "Where was I?"

"Ha! Like life interrupted, right?" Eric said.

"Yeah, like I thought somehow, we would fight through all the thicket and brambles to where we could see the sky. The dark clouds are gone. Being back home, it's a little closer."

"It took a lifetime, Dad," Alana said, "but we're closer. We're closer."

* * *

Kathryn and I set about making the house ours again. Linda had to be in Washington for weeks to close her practice there, and then in North Carolina for several months to help Alana and her husband, Ben, care for our new granddaughter. Eric was pursuing his graduate program in energy and environment at a Midwestern university.

On the first Christmas home, Eric joined Kathryn and me in Berkeley while Linda was with Alana's family. On the night before Christmas, I took Eric and Kathryn to Union Square in San Francisco. Christmas wreaths decorated each window in the ten floors of the Macy's building. White lights sparkled off the trees and around the skating rink at the square. We sat, had a glass of wine, and watched the skaters swirl around the rink. The Christmas atmosphere was festive and lively. Later, we went for dinner.

In the warm, bustling café, a bit of tenseness settled over the dinner table. Kathryn exuded her usual conviviality at Christmas time, but Eric surprised me. He was a little stiff, though polite. I sensed a growing irritation in Eric. For one thing, prior to leaving home, Kathryn had delayed our departure by over an hour to do her swimming workout. Kathryn's usual slow pace—perusing the menu, ordering foods, eating—put her out of sync with Eric and me. Additionally, Eric was coping with a broken romance and struggling alone in graduate school.

We returned to Berkeley for an after-dinner drink at the home where Kathryn and Eric started life thirty years earlier. I was happy to have at least two of the kids together. Especially these two. With their mother and Alana in the east, I was hoping our time together would lay the groundwork for rebuilding a sense of home back in Berkeley, for getting a little closer to each other now that they were adults. But the coolness at dinner grew worse as we gathered for our nightcap.

The house lights were low. Candles gave off a soft glow around our kitchen island. Kathryn kept Eric and me waiting.

Eric groaned, "She's been constantly checking her phone messages and now probably primping in her room."

After more than twenty minutes, she at last joined us around the island. Eric glared at his sister. She sat across from him, innocent and unsuspecting. I sensed Eric's frustration and anger building. Kathryn had kept us waiting just as she always had done, but this time Eric wasn't prepared to be gracious. It was one straw too many for him.

"Why do we always have to wait for you?" Eric asked.

"What's your problem?" Kathryn said, tilting her head back, eyebrows furrowed.

"We've waited for you three times today," he blurted out.

"You don't have to wait. You could get started," she replied.

"You don't understand, Kathryn." Eric's voice rose. "I had to wait for you all my life. I couldn't ever tell you how angry I was."

"Sure you could," she replied in a totally innocent manner, not reading the tidal wave building in her brother. "Just say something. Bada bing. We can talk about it."

"No. No, I couldn't," Eric retorted. "I could never do that." A jet of steam had started to escape. "You wouldn't have understood."

"OK. So, I'm late sometimes. But I never forget birthdays and anniversaries," she offered. "I'm the best at that, right Dad?" She glanced at me for support. "Like for example, the date your father died, your mother—right, Dad?"

"Yes, Kathryn, you are great at that," I acknowledged. Kathryn had a knack for remembering anniversaries and birthdays, but she had major problems remembering recent information—conversations with people in her life, about agreements, and plans—information that is easily recallable for most people. Kathryn had learned to use her iPhone to keep track of such things. Worse still, Kathryn had become increasingly blind to the impact of her behaviors, like tardiness and unnecessary delays.

"You don't know what it was like for me, Kathryn," Eric said. He pressed his hand into his chest. The door swung further open. "I could never have my own friends over to the house. I didn't get all the attention that you got. I was pushed aside or forgotten. Mom and Dad had to take care of you." Eric's face was growing redder. "I had to play ball on your field."

Kathryn was caught by surprise. "I don't see why you haven't mentioned this before," she said, in a quiet defensive tone.

"I could never say anything. I wasn't allowed to." Eric's words came out like cutting gravel. They had been lying dormant for more than a decade. Now they were erupting fast and hard. He was standing now, his hands on the island as he stared down at her.

Kathryn was at the edge of buckling under Eric's attack. She shrank back, cowering under the storm. Tears welled in her eyes. She still didn't seem to be comprehending what was behind his assault. Her lip curled up. Her eyes were searching, her face long and sad. I felt a deep hurt in my heart for her.

The suffering on her face threw me back to the pediatric intensive care ward thirty years earlier. Her face was quivering, her mouth open and gasping. My first impulse was to save her somehow, to block Eric's piercing attack. Balanced against this reflex was my growing recognition that it was time to stay back. Lower the shield a bit. Despite the energy in Eric's onslaught, she needed to hear this, to be aware of her impact on him over all these years. But I was afraid the confrontation would spiral into freefall.

I tried to keep her engaged. An image flashed before my eyes of me preparing to tell Alana about her grandfather's death when she was three.

"You see, Kathryn," I started, my mouth dry, my confidence gone, "Eric didn't ever feel like he could criticize you. You sometimes don't understand situations. Like when you open presents at Christmas or your birthday, you take a super extra-long time. We all have to wait for you. Or when you don't understand the plan for the day, Eric or somebody always had to explain it. You're always the last one in and the last one out the door."

Kathryn stared down at the table, trying to comprehend what she was being told. The message was plain enough but it didn't seem to hit home for her. She had clearly never registered this reaction before. She wiped tears from her eyes. She was glimpsing a world, Eric's world, she never knew existed. Seemingly not knowing whether to apologize or fight back, she withdrew.

"You need to know that Eric has had to bottle this up most of his life. It's not fair to you now, and maybe you don't understand, but you had a profound effect on Eric's life."

She was silent, appearing to collapse inside.

I continued, trying to soften the delivery, to give her a

sense that we still loved her, that she wasn't being attacked by me as well.

"Eric's built up anger over many years. He has never been able to externalize it, to tell you directly. It's coming out now."

Blinking, she couldn't seem to find words. Then I turned to Eric, trying to referee a bit.

"Eric, you have to see that Kathryn doesn't understand. She's never seen any of your anger. It's not entirely her fault." Eric stared at the table, drawing in a deep breath.

Kathryn glanced at me. A light wave of relief flowed over her face.

"Kathryn, you see it's important for Eric to voice his anger."

"But why hasn't he ever said anything before?" she asked again, her voice hardly audible.

"He couldn't, Kathryn. It wouldn't have made sense to you. And he didn't feel he could attack you. You're old enough now, and I think you are mature enough, to see his side."

She shifted in her chair, looked at the ceiling as she often did when at a loss, and then down to the table. Her eyes avoided ours. She took out her earrings, slowly, as if buying time. She cupped them in her hands and rose from her stool and walked slowly out of the room.

Eric and I sat in silence. Three castaways hit by fierce winds all coming from the same cyclone. Eric had his head on his arm, weeping quietly. He rocked back on his stool and took a deep breath.

"This had to happen sooner or later," I said. "It was good for her to see it; painful, but it had to happen somehow."

"I know, Dad," he said. He looked up and into my eyes. "I can feel your guilt."

He was right. Eric wasn't protected enough from Kathryn's needs. Neither Linda nor I fully appreciated the mental energy that Eric had to expend as a teen just to hold position. On the other hand, we had no option in the daily triaging of family needs other than to give Kathryn first attention. As an early teen when he was shown to have a high IQ, I took comfort that Eric would somehow be able to handle things. But by then, the damage was done. Too often, he was left to his own devices and, except perhaps for video games, had no outlet for his frustrations. I worried that the storm he had to endure would drive him away from having kids.

This was a moment, like a growing number of others, when being a father required skilled arbitration more than rulemaking. The kids were adults. They were beginning to define their own challenges and solutions, and they sometimes came into conflict. In the following days, a half dozen sessions with Kathryn were not enough to explain why Eric unloaded on her. To this day, she is still puzzled.

* * *

Signal moments of change appeared in Eric over the ensuing year and gradually formed a shift in his attitude toward Kathryn. The first bits of evidence came in small trickles. He phoned to tell me that he was thinking about getting Kathryn a bicycle. Eric had started a side business, buying old bikes at auction, fixing them up, and selling them. The bike business itself was an interesting development, a venturing out to gain a little extra cash while searching for work. At first, I saw his gesture as a way to compensate her for his Christmas attack. In any case, to think about his sister, and to devote a bicycle to her, was a new and welcome gesture of goodwill that couldn't have been predicted at that Christmas flareup. He had always been thoughtful and clever when it came to gifts, always appropriate, usually unexpected, and invariably prized by the recipient. But there was no special occasion about the bicycle idea for his sister. Whether a "let's make up" or purely a gesture of kindness, it was utterly opposite from that Christmas meltdown.

A half year later, he called to say that he had arranged for a surprise for Kathryn's birthday. He had obtained tickets for the two of them to attend a 49ers–Redskins game. Eric was also making plans for a birthday banner for her at the stadium. Despite having lived in the Washington area for years, Kathryn was a great fan of the 49ers. The team represented her home and she was thrilled with the gift.

Perhaps the most remarkable moment of the Eric shift— I'm going to call it transformation to proto-parenthood—was not that he became a father, but that he took on a parental role between Linda and me just as Alana had done years earlier.

As this book was taking shape, I circulated a draft to the family. Linda objected to certain portrayals of her. We fussed about it for a while and, having already sent Eric a copy, I texted him to get his input about whether I had been fair to his mom. Was the story balanced? He texted back a few comments and then called. We had a level, man-to-man talk. He offered fresh insights. He suggested I beef up mom's positive role a bit to put more balance in the story. I took his suggestions onboard.

I didn't know it at the time, but right after the incident, he phoned Linda, who was traveling at the time, to explain that Dad had screwed up, but that it was only a draft, and afterall, that's what drafts are for. I only found out about his call much later. Still, it was exactly the right move to reassure Linda, and it worked perfectly for me, too. Later, Linda and I both admired the way Eric had handled his adult "children."

Eric leapt forward before our very eyes. He had benefited from therapy and persistent work to decode his anxiety and defuse his anger. He had broken through. He had stepped in with a deft touch to stave off a bit of threat here, to encourage a bit of support there. Eric was not only doing his part to hold up the sky, he was also adding to the sky. Eric was putting pieces of the sky back in place on his own. Above all, I, as Dad, wasn't needed for that work any longer.

* * *

At the same time, that difficult Christmas night marked a new glimmer in my fathering. I glimpsed a light at the end of a tunnel. With the sky-holding business now pretty much obsolete, another phase of fatherhood was upon me. Life had pushed me forward to a new point on the arc of fatherhood. Some of the arrows in my quiver—modulating the Phantom, listening, comforting—needed to be replaced. The stakes had shifted from survival to emotional well-being, from uncertainty in their future to trust in one another. My role needed to be more one of mentor, to show the ups and downs of family conflicts, and to remind the kids about where they had come from and where they were going. It was time to reflect outwardly with them about decisions and risk-taking, about their inner drives. It was time to point to the benefits and pitfalls of protecting and being protected.

THREE BODIES IN SYNC

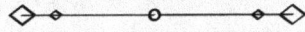

My writing sessions, whether memoir or essays on cities, had a certain rhythm. I would fly on the keyboard, crafting this chapter or that. Then, pushing away from the desk, I would clear the kinks in my back, turn up Pink Floyd, and dance my way into the kitchen to wash the dishes lying in the sink. This urge for cleansing went with the writing. I used to muse that washing and writing were essentially the same thing, except I was still looking for the suds in my writing, whereas I had already found the order in the sentence of dirty dishes.

Inevitably, I shuffled back to my corner office and, like some Newtonian machine with flywheel still spinning, picked up the pieces of the paragraph left dangling. I was propelled along with the tropical energy of Sulawesi and molasses, choosing which direction I should take next: Another blog about cities in the developing world, or an essay to capture the three bodies in sync—my three kids arcing through life, aiming to find their own destinies?

Alana was flourishing in her chosen world, having become

a mom and research faculty member in neuroscience at a major university. She imposed rules on her little one in a fashion partly reminiscent of my father—firm and with no second guessing. Yet, she was never harsh. She had confidence and a light, loving touch.

At work, she plowed her way through mounds of brain-wave data recorded from electrodes on subjects ("they're 'participants,' Dad."). The data she obtained were displayed as multiple squiggles on a printout. They trace an inner, mental reality no one can fathom without heavy doses of statistics. She had a profound knowledge of how the brain works. Her deep grasp of the way people learn and patterns of behavior enriched her mothering.

She received a grant award from a national foundation honoring the most promising young scientists conducting neurobiological research. Only innovative, cutting-edge projects get funded. Hers was one. The thirty years since the rivet scene under the bridge seemed to have passed in a wink. On a visit after her award, I sat with her at a picnic table near her university. I watched her sketch out a research program with calm assurance, diagramming on paper the conceptual approach and operational steps she would take. It was like watching an artist place vibrant color on a canvas.

Meanwhile, Kathryn was now living with Linda and me. Her days were filled with an anxiety about not being with her boyfriend, George, back in Washington, DC. He was a complicated guy whose own disabilities exacerbated, rather than offset, her own. They were reaching the limits of a long-distance relationship.

"I keep having 'missing' feelings," Kathryn had said routinely. She moped around, barely managing to keep to her daily routine of working in the afternoon at an elementary school's extended day center.

I urged her to enroll at one of the nearby community colleges in Berkeley, to meet new people, make a life in the West. She finally found a course that fit her needs, but as we drew closer to the first day of school, Kathryn's anxiety grew more intense—it was practically paralytic by the opening of classes. George had been leaning on her to return east. She loved California but felt she should not give up on him.

Eric had reached the end of his graduate program, finishing his last term paper. Though much of the hardest grunt work was done, the third draft with lots of unfinished sections came in over email. "Dad, please take a look at this. It's too short and I've run aground," his email read. I saw that he had made good progress, but had strayed from the topic here and there.

"Stay with the central idea," I suggested.

"Got it, thnx," he wrote back. After a short session on the phone and some comments online, he set to work once again.

Later in the day, Kathryn finished her afternoon work at a daycare for toddlers and was at a pool, swimming off her anxiety. I knew she was upset; her mind was repeatedly going over the cognitive dissonance she was suffering. Pressure from her boyfriend for not being with him in DC on the one hand, and on the other the haranguing from me about starting a new life in Berkeley. Her memory loss, comprehension issues, and my persistent admonitions created a whirlpool of endless indecision about the move-or-stay question.

As I settled in for the evening, I found that Alana had sent me a Father's Day gift, an online edition of the TV drama *Newsroom*. I regarded that show, much like *West Wing*, as a buffer between the viewer and real life, a way to engage in and hear about the issues of the day without having to deal with reality. The too-clever TV dialogue was delivered in a polished, dramatic fashion which is controlled, well-performed, has a clincher of an ending, and can be shut off when it's over, leaving the viewer with a satisfying sense of closure. Despite Alana's urging, I had consistently and conveniently forgotten to find a *Newsroom* episode on my own, and now with the Father's Day gift sitting in front of me, I couldn't shirk it any longer. I launched the program.

As *Newsroom* played on my screen, the fourth draft of Eric's piece came pinging by email. With the TV still on, I turned to Eric's opening paragraphs and saw that he had really nailed it, setting the stage for his paper. He had doubled the length and executed the finishing touches smoothly. I immediately called him (*Newsroom* was running in the background) and gave him an oral high five. As I was talking to him, and the *Newsroom* principal characters were falling in love again, Kathryn appeared quietly in my office, her eyes red. She laid her head on my shoulder and wept softly.

That was the picture of three kids in sync on Father's Day: Phone in left hand with Eric, TV *Newsroom* episode from Alana on the screen in front of me, Kathryn weeping softly on right shoulder.

Eric's analytics had broken the back of the challenge; Kathryn was weeping because she knew that no matter what she did, she would put somebody off—either her boyfriend or her parents; Newsroom dramatically coming to a close. I was congratulating Eric for a fantastic job, feeling great about Alana having given me a good piece of drama for Fathers' Day, and softly suggesting to Kathryn that he was not the only man on the planet. Goodbye and congrats, Eric. Switch off Newsroom and thank you, Alana. Kathryn, you must do what you feel is right, even if he is not our choice.

They will not have the lives I tried to steer for them. They will find their own paths, just as I followed a path through demonstrations at Berkeley, the Peace Corps in Costa Rica, and a professional career on urban poverty in the developing world. Those and other choices my father did not always understand but would cheer in his later years. And shouldn't that be me, cheering for my kids as I pick up the beat of their rhythms, now that they're out on their own?

* * *

One evening, several months after Kathryn had jumped off the fence to move to DC, the phone rang.

"I'm not coming back, Dad." Kathryn's declaration came resolutely over the phone. Not coming back, the one who as an infant was given a one-in-ten chance of survival, the one who was told she wouldn't graduate from high school, the one who found her own jobs. After a year living with Linda and me, a year of trying to steer her away from George's dysfunctional personality, we had relented and had let her go. Kathryn had a dozen close friends in DC who were caring and supportive of her.

Finally, she did it. She moved and confronted him.

"I want more," she told us she had said to him.

"I'm giving all I can," was the reply.

"That's not enough," she said. Three weeks later, she had met someone else and was dating again.

A couple of months passed. On one of our nearly daily phone chats, Alana said, "You know, Dad, she has no business being where she is right now."

"Yeah, we shouldn't have let her go back to DC," I said.

"No, no. That's not what I mean," Alana replied. "I mean her state in the world. Think about it, Dad," Alana continued. "Given all that she went through these past decades, almost any scenario that we could've imagined is worse than what actually happened."

She was right. I thought about all the theories of personality development, disability, and social change. Some say change depends on where you start, others say the most important things are the inputs and forces that are exerted along the way. Still others refer to unpredictable influences—like the butterfly effect in chaos theory—that exert small changes in one part of the world and end up creating giant outcomes far away. And then there are the intrinsic qualities of Kathryn herself. Pure drive. I guess you could say by extension the same was true for Alana and Eric. Each had to manage their own albatrosses around their necks for thirty years. Eric had a high performing older sister and a super challenging younger one, not to mention his own burdens of disability. Alana had a different but no lighter load.

Kathryn declared her independence with, "I'm not coming back." Alana did it, too, years earlier with "Shut the fuck up." Then, most recently, Eric had reprimanded me for stepping into a conversation he was having about jobs the science convention in San Diego. "You have to leave it to me," he had said. I didn't like any of those statements, but I can now see them all as declarations of independence. All were signal moments in their becoming something new, getting out from under past shadows, and chalking out their own future.

When Kathryn announced that she wasn't coming back, I ran a victory lap in my heart, while breaking out in a flood of tears—not from relief that she had made it, but from my selfish sadness of losing her to the outside world. She was on her own. And she had made that decision herself. What better reward than to see her act that way?

* * *

I was traveling the arc of fatherhood. The idyllic model I started with Alana hovers like a distant dream, beautiful while it lasted. All I could see in the first few years after Kathryn's hospitalization was the physical threat—a throwback from my Phantom Captain, who had saved me in my younger years from traumatic physical encounters. After Kathryn's illness, the instinct of physical survival had burst forth, and practically took over. My arms went to the sky to protect my family from lightning strikes. With time, that physical Phantom melded into a metaphorical one. Holding up the sky became a practice of conservatism, of being on the cautious side of decisions, even when my kids wanted to take risks, like Eric at the rocket launch or Alana at the Dead concert, or Kathryn on the cruise ship dance floor.

At the middle of the arc was an insight about finding a softer magic in fathering—of identifying emotional angles and bringing them out of the shadows in my relationship with my kids. To talk about their fears and mine, to work through them, to make them a part of our bond. That was the nuance of fathering I had hoped to achieve. With it came a rich closeness and mutual trust that I relish with my children now.

In the end, the main thing was to understand and manage my gut reactions, to be present with the kids, to support them the whole way, to discover their changing needs, and to adapt. At the same time, I had to hold down my differences with Linda and to shine light on those values we shared.

CHAIN OF LESSONS

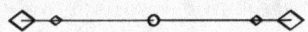

As the heat of the summer fell upon me, I called to mind once again that photo of father and son observing their home going up in flames during the North Bay fire. After traveling the arc of fatherhood, my skies are much less clouded, although spotted areas of doubt remain. Many times, I played through imaginary conversations I wished I'd had with Dad to clear away nagging discomfort. We never came to closure about that getting-girls-pregnant scene, the gasoline can incident, and Dad resenting my softer side.

I pictured Dad and me sitting on our porch, hoping to move beyond my anger and guilt, aiming for the calm that comes with the passage of time, and imagine our conversation.

"Dad, as tough as you were on me, I sometimes think that you would've been a better father for my kids than I was for them."

Dad looked a bit astonished. He gazed up to the sky as he often did, his fisherman's cap and his beefy frame still in place in his senior years. "You mean, stricter rules, no excuses?" He paused. "Maybe, son," he replied, softly. "You did get a little wobbly."

If only he could have delivered to Kent and me more flexibility in his rules, express them more clearly, and pull back from his gruff exterior. And if only I could have relayed his rules to my kids straight up. Instead, they heard from me the imperfect echoes of my dad's guidance, distorted by not ever having trusted my dad, not ever having fully trusted myself as a rule maker, and me trying to integrate the calculus of disability and the specter of the Phantom into every fatherly decision. Trying so hard to hold up the sky, to not be aggressive and rough, to anticipate and foil the overcautiousness of the Phantom, looking to plumb the depths of emotional understanding, I got lost. I lost track of the most important north star: Trust in myself but keep the rules clear. Don't make excuses. If only, if, if.

I said, "It's like, you were too cautious, but you never got confused about giving direction like I did. You had no choice, your father gone and all, never knowing if there would be food on the table."

"Yes, I suppose," he answered. "But I had to deny my soft side, just like you denied your hard side. For me there was no room to be soft. But I could see at Kathryn's bedside, the night I died, that you were going to have a very different row to hoe," he said.

"And that's the problem. My kids really needed a fixed guide, like you—consistent and repeated affirmation, no two ways about it, no do-overs or bending of the rules."

"Don't be so hard on yourself, son." I pictured him now with his arm around my shoulder. "We need to acknowledge our mistakes rather than pretend perfection." We sat silently for a moment. "Besides, Alana and Kathryn are doing fine. Your loving instincts with them worked well."

I drew a deep breath. "Yeah, that was easy and strong with Alana. She was a rivet right from the get-go. But with Eric, it's a different story, not because he's a guy, but because he had a double load—on the one hand, Kathryn always pulling him back, and on the other, he had his own disabilities. My empathy with his constant battling to reach a level playing field didn't provide him the tools he really needed. He could have used a little more of that NASA-style scripting of a playbook." I began to tear up. "I was always off balance. Now, I worry that he may just opt out of fatherhood."

"So what?" Dad shot back softly. "He succeeded, and grandly. And he's strong enough to make his own decisions about being a father. Besides, your kids, as parents or not, will have to solve the puzzles you created for them, the puzzles that arise from the solutions to problems I created for you. That's inevitable. You thought you had to hold up the sky, to protect Kathryn and Eric from their disabilities. That's understandable, but not realistic. One thing's vital: Don't underestimate the legacy of love, resilience, and emotional strength you provided for your kids."

Dad got up from his chair and walked to the end of the porch lost deep in thought, then came back, stopping in front of me. "New dads always struggle to correct problems created by their dads. I had that challenge big time." Dad was at his most sympathetic self. "My dad deserted us; you stuck with it. You gave your kids something extremely valuable. They trusted you, even if you were uncertain and felt always behind the curve with Eric."

Yes. The trust, at least that.

The tissue of trust had grown out of my hit-and-miss efforts at probing my kids' emotional lives. My gestures were often clumsy, but authentic, like Kathryn's wooden fish and coaching Eric in baseball and warning him about the Steinbeck story. At other times, they were just natural and deep, as in the "Box of Rain" with Alana. Over time, my connections with the kids grew thicker and more reliable. The kids counted on me for advice, a friendly ear, and emotional support.

We paused, silent for a moment. Dad said: "I regret that we never got that trust thing going between us." He looked into my eyes. "I guess I was just forged in a different crucible. I never got to daddy school. For me, life was a long march in survival school . . . you know, the 1919 fire, my father having abandoned us . . . Your grandmother struggling to keep us afloat, then the Depression. Those events cast a long shadow."

"I get it, Dad. That environment was also a nursery for your Phantom Captain. He overwhelmed you. Yes, he kept you safe, allowed you to provide for us, but he also got in the way of our getting close. But we're getting past that now, Dad. And I can forgive you."

The lessons of fatherhood were now cropping up in crisp display, too late to make use of them but maybe helpful to pass along to the kids and certainly helpful for me to come to closure with my dad. Lessons have arced across time. My dad fighting through the uncertainty and fear of a fatherless home; me, tiptoeing around or running for cover under Dad's overbearing pressure. Then me as a father, turning myself into an empathetic softy for the kids always reaching for the sky. Then, my kids as parents, appreciating our mutual trust but reacting to my squishiness, and hardening up for their kids.

The journey of this book has helped me to see my fatherly foibles as well as to find closure with my dad and to forgive him. Maybe the book will also help my kids to forgive me and see ways to smooth out the endless chain of reactions that shape parenting across generations.

EPILOGUE

Alana and Eric currently live in the Eastern time zone. Alana recently gave us grandchild number two and continues directing an EEG lab at a leading university. Eric works in energy and the environment at a major consulting firm and is actively shaping a future in his field. Kathryn lives near us, manages her affairs mostly independently, and works steadily with toddlers in an after-school program. Every day, she uses up all her energy.

As the kids build their own lives as adults, Linda and I have launched a new phase of ours. We started to travel more and began sailing. Our adventures at sea brought many experiences of working out problems on the sailboat together—without the kids—providing therapy we had needed for years. Those sailing experiences built a quiet sense of accomplishment and renewed confidence. We began to accept our circumstances, our differences, and the strength we had together. With that acceptance came recognition of decades of deeply buried sorrow, of fighting against the reality of our lives, of trying not just to make things better, but to repair the past. We found joy again.

We began to meld our personal styles into a more unified whole—not as perfect parents, not the perfect couple—but as a richly rewarding partnership. The children's achievements were already showing that we had accomplished a lot of what we had hoped for all along.

The commitment Linda and I made to stay together despite the storm of bad luck was forged at a moment more than forty years ago. Then, as we stood over Kathryn's hospital bed as she lay on the doorway of death, we vowed to give her our all. We followed that pledge with Eric and Alana, as well. We stayed together not just for the sake of the kids, but also because we recognized that we had been hit by a streak of very bad luck and that shouldn't—and didn't—undo the reasons we fell in love in the first place. We recognized in the beginning, and honor to this day, an enduring love and a deep and unbreakable respect for one another's strengths. We will celebrate our fiftieth wedding anniversary this year.

END